The New York Times
Captive Vocabulary

By Robert Greenman

To Carol

Published by The New York Times
229 West 43d Street,
New York, N.Y. 10036

Copyright © 1980, 1982, The New York Times Co.

*All rights reserved. No part of this book may
be reproduced in any form or by an electronic
or mechanical means, including information storage
and retrieval systems, without permission in writing
from the publisher, except by a reviewer who may
quote brief passages in a review. Address inquiries
to: College and School Service, The New York Times.*

**Library of Congress
Cataloging in Publication Data**

Greenman, Robert.
    The New York Times Captive Vocabulary.

1. Vocabulary.   I. New York Times.   II. Title.
PE1449.G67 428.1   80-21741
ISBN 0-8129-0974-7

Manufactured in the United States of America

Cartoons by Fred Fredericks

Introduction

In my journalism classes at James Madison High School, *The New York Times* has always been required reading. With it I have taught my students every aspect of journalism, from reporting and reviewing to editorial writing and humor, from the art of headline writing to the business of advertising. *The Times* has even sparked most of our discussions of journalistic ethics, invasion of privacy, and libel laws.

Although it takes my eleventh grade journalism students several days to become familiar with the layout and daily sections of *The Times,* and to lose their fear of what they previously thought was a paper for eggheads, they soon find *The Times* a far more readable paper than they had imagined.

One aspect of the paper that continued to give them some difficulty, though, was its vocabulary. *The Times,* indeed, did use a wider selection of words than other newspapers, and for eleventh graders this meant that each day they would run across several in *The Times* that they were unfamiliar with. In many cases, they could figure out a word's general meaning from its context. In other cases, they would completely miss the writer's point if they didn't know a word's definition.

I abandoned teaching them vocabulary from a textbook and instead asked them to start keeping a card file of words along with the sentences they appeared in and their definitions. I cautioned them to be sure their dictionary definitions fit each word as it was used in their particular sentence, since almost every word has more than one meaning. For example, if they came across "veneer" as a description of a person's outward behavior, they shouldn't write down its definition as "the outer finished surface of a piece of wood or other material."

When I collected their first batch of cards (twenty-five each from forty students), I discovered that among those thousand cards, many words appeared over and over again, but in different sentences, and from every section of *The Times*. I realized that while *The Times* did present a wide variety of "vocabulary" words, by reading the paper daily my students would meet most of them over and over again, and slowly but surely master them all.

Realizing that a book of these words, along with sample sentences, could be of enormous help to student readers of *The Times,* and a valuable book for their teachers, I proposed the idea to *Times* executives.

They liked the idea. In fact, for several years they had suspected that there was a core of words used over and over again in *The Times* which could easily be mastered by any steady *Times* reader, and that an awareness of this would help disprove the notion that *The Times* is "hard to read." They even had a phrase for this core of words — "The Captive Vocabulary," words indispensable to *Times* writers as they went about explaining, describing, reviewing and persuading.

But why produce this book with only students in mind, said Marjorie Longley, *The Times* Director of Public Affairs. Even adult readers would enjoy browsing through a treasure house of *Times* words and sentences, she said, adding that a great many adult readers, too, must also come across words whose meanings they do not know or are not sure of.

With every *Times* reader in mind, therefore, I set about collecting the words and sentences for this book. For eight weeks, from June 10 to August 4, 1979, I read *The Times* from first page to last, gathering from every section of the weekday and Sunday sections, except the Book Review and Magazine, "The Captive Vocabulary."

I typed up a separate file card for each word and the sentence it appeared in, and in some cases accumulated several cards with the same word, so I could choose for the book the sentence that best showed the word in its most common *Times* usage.

During the first three weeks, I gathered between forty and sixty new words a day. After three weeks, I was taking fewer than fifteen new words a day, because most of what I was now seeing were repeats. Seeing the first weeks' words appearing over and over again, I had already proven to myself that there was, indeed, a *Times* "captive vocabulary." And there it was, literally, in my file box.

In eight weeks I came across fewer than two dozen words that were not regularly used in *The Times,* words like *internecine, orotund* and *troglodyte.* I ended up with 1,200 words that I considered *The Times* "captive vocabulary," and reduced that number to a little over 1,000 for the purposes of this book.

Most of the sentences appearing here were written by *Times* staff writers, but a good number appeared in Op-Ed articles and in freelance material. Some appeared in quotes

abate   uh•BAYT
(diminish)

The booing did not abate when Gil Flores pinch-hit for Ellis and singled to center for the Met's first run and only their fifth in 46 innings.

aberration   a•buh•RAY•shuhn
(departure from the norm)

An aberration that has appeared in a few collections, notably those of Nina Ricci and Hubert de Givenchy, is the return of the bustle.

abet   uh•BET
(encourage)

General Somoza must finally admit that his refusal to yield power is abetting radicalism, not preventing it.

abeyance   uh•BAY•ance
(temporary suspension)

But plans for substantially increasing Saudi Arabia's production capacity in the years ahead seem to have fallen into abeyance.

abhor   uhb•HOR
(detest)

"On the contrary," he said, "the public clearly abhors any kind of terrorism against anyone. There may be terrorists in Turkey who intend to try to destroy our relations with our allies, but this should not be confused with public opinion."

abiding
(lasting)   uh•BUY•ding

"The charm, the structure of the story, the pace of the prose come through even in English," and he mentioned Mr. Singer's abiding concern that the English of the stories might be right.

abomination
(anything hateful and disgusting)   uh•BOM•uh•nay•shuhn

There are some "hasty" foods in this world that I consider culinary abominations. I would count among them instant rice and the frozen dinners that abound on the freezer shelves of supermarkets.

ABOMINATION

abort
(cut short)   uh•BORT

Back at Mission Control, some thought the landing might have to be aborted. But a young computer specialist named Stephen Bayles assured space officials and Mr. Armstrong that everything was all right.

abound
(to be plentiful)   uh•BOUND

Hopes abound that better management, such as the imposition of odd-even sales days, might ease the gas lines somewhat.

abrasive uh•BRAY•siv
(rubbing people the wrong way)

An abrasive personality is not necessarily a bar to a woman's advancement in academia, business or politics, a study by Dr. Florence L. Denmark, president of the American Psychological Association, has concluded.

absolve uhb•ZOLV
(to free from responsibility for)

Most guaranteed contracts that exist in baseball today have clauses absolving the team of paying the remainder of the contract if the player is killed while flying a plane himself.

abysmal uh•BIZ•muhl
(immeasurably bad)

We found that, just as in the United States, the quality of health-care services abroad can range from excellent to abysmal.

abyss uh•BISS
(a bottomless depth)

"We are far apart," he said. "There is a great abyss between the two sides. I'm on a little rail fence somewhere in the middle."

academician
a•ka•duh•MI•shuhn
(a teacher or administrator of high scholarly attainments)

Several nationally prominent academicians testified at the hearing, as did the children who sued the school district.

accolade
AK•uh•layd
(high praise)

If I were to own a restaurant, I think that the last accolade I would want is to have it dubbed the best in the world.

accreditation
uh•kre•di•TAY•shuhn
(certification for having met certain standards)

Hospitals are now required to have radioisotope, or nuclear medicine facilities to meet accreditation standards.

acerbic
uh•SER•bik
(bitingly sharp)

She, however, is smarter and more sensible than he will ever be, and she has the last acerbic word in every argument.

acquiescent
ak•we•ESS•ent
(consenting without protest)

But, evidently reflecting the frustration felt by many officials, Mr. Carter told reporters last Sunday that he could not "see how the rest of the world can sit back in an acquiescent state and accept unrestrained and unwarranted increases in OPEC oil prices."

acrid
AK•rid
(stinging or irritating to the taste or smell)

The tunnel, its floor thick with oozing mud and its air pungent with the acrid odor of blasting powder, rang with the scream of the diesel-powered earth loaders.

acrimonious   ac•ruh•MO•nee•us
(bitter and harsh)

Early in the Carter Administration, an acrimonious feud between ACTION director Sam Brown and Peace Corps head Carolyn Payton became public.

acronym   AK•ruh•nim
(a word formed from the first — or first few — letters of a series of words)

The company is Jordache Jeans Inc., an acronym for Joseph, Ralph and Avi with a more Parisian-sounding "che" on the end, that was organized in March 1978.

acumen   uh•KYOO•men
(keenness and quickness in understanding and dealing with a situation)

They noted that, while he had lost nothing of his acumen, Mr. Meany's physical appearance had declined noticeably over the last year.

acute   uh•KYOOT
(critical)

Authoritative industry sources said that Iran's giant Soviet-built steel complex at Isfahan might be forced to close in less than two weeks because of an acute shortage of coking coal.

adamant   AD•uh•muhnt
(unyielding)

At age 35, Mrs. King is adamant about two things besides winning: thinking positive and having fun.

ADAMANT

adjacent uh•JAY•suhnt
(next to; nearby)

In past years the beaches and the adjacent amusement area have drawn more than a million people on the Fourth of July holiday.

admonition ad•mo•NI•shuhn
(advice or a warning to correct a fault)

He was a heavy smoker, first of cigarettes and then pipes, following admonitions against smoking by doctors.

adulation ad•jeh•LAY•shun
(excessive praise)

Finally, he decided that the real Reggie Jackson had "a sense of values" that have nothing to do with all the adulation and all the money that are his.

advent AD•vent
(arrival)

With the advent of the live vaccine in 1963, measles cases began a steady decline until 1974, when there were 22,094 cases.

adventurism ad•VEN•cher•iz•em
(actions or tactics, esp. in politics or international relations, that are regarded as recklessly daring and involving the risk of serious consequences)

What the United States regards as "adventurism" — Soviet support for Marxist governments that came to power by force in Ethiopia, Angola and Afghanistan — the Russians view as legitimate, principled assistance to anti-imperialist movements of national liberation.

affable AF•uh•buhl
(friendly)

A slight, balding and affable man, he is a potential Senate candidate in 1980.

affinity
(a natural liking or sympathy)   uh•FIN•i•tea

Harry, Teresa and Tom Meyerhoff, the owners of Spectacular Bid, decided to stick with Franklin because "the horse and the jockey have an affinity for each other."

affluent
(wealthy)   AF•loo•int

Long before the jet age, a grand tour — a tour of the Continent in high style — was considered by the affluent to be a basic part of one's upbringing.

affront
(an insult or offense against one's dignity, intelligence, etc.)   uh•FRONT

Earl Lindquist of Houston, a 54-year-old contractor, is affronted by what he regards as the "packaging" of the President: "I'm telling you, it doesn't matter how Jimmy parts his hair or shakes his fist, the Government is beneath words."

aficionado
(a devoted follower of some sport, art, etc.)   uh•fee•syuh•NAH•doh

"Most all of the people who do swim nude or sunbathe in a social setting enjoy seeing other people nude," conceded Gerald Morsello, 40, a Eugene, Ore. bus driver and nude-beach aficionado.

aftermath
(a result or consequence, esp. an unpleasant one)   AF•ter•math

Because of trash-collection problems in the aftermath of the tugboat strike, alternate-side parking regulations will be in effect today in Manhattan and Brooklyn only.

aggravate
(make worse, intensify)   AG•ruh•vayt

The accelerating use of mechanical harvesters has aggravated a long battle between California growers and the United Farm Workers of America, the union led by Cesar Chavez.

agile A•jil
(quick and easy of movement)
Mrs. Lloyd, who lost to the 22-year-old Czechoslovak when they last played three months ago, dispelled all doubts of her ability to master the grass surface. She moved agilely and came to the net confidently on short shots.

aggregation AG•ruh•gay•shuhn
(grouping)
An unusual aggregation of drummers will be assembled tonight at Carnegie Hall by Mr. Gillespie.

alfresco al•FRESS•ko
(outdoor)
The afternoon alfresco dances and music are free, but reservations for the banquet, unfortunately, are no longer available.

allegory AL•uh•gaw•ree
(a story in which people, things and happenings have a hidden or symbolic meaning)
This was a painting of "The Dance of Death," a common medieval pictorial representation of the allegorical figure of Death leading all—the highborn and the low—to the same fate.

alleviate uh•LEE•vee•ayt
(lessen)
A modest supply of gasoline is expected to be made available this week to dealers in New York, New Jersey and Connecticut to alleviate what officials said yesterday was a worsening shortage.

aloof
uh•LOOF

(reserved; cool)

Once, when I could not find a taxi to take me to White City Stadium, I got my pole on to the subway. To appear under the earth with 16 feet of pole draws attention. Even the most aloof turn a curious eye.

ALOOF

altercation
all•ter•KAY•shun

(an angry or heated argument)

"We are not happy that our employees were involved in this altercation with the Cosmos," said Les Unger, a spokesman for the Meadowlands. "They are hired to clean the stands and that's what they should be doing."

alumna
uh•LUHM•nuh

(female graduate)

The bride is an alumna of the Garrison Forest School and Wheaton College in Norton, Mass.

alumnus
uh•LUM•nuss

(male graduate)

Mr. Salas is an alumnus of the Hotchkiss School and Harvard College.

ambiguous
am•BIG•yoo•uhs

(uncertain)

Music appears to occupy an ambiguous position in Islamic culture. Instrumental music was forbidden by Islamic orthodoxy, although the use of drums was allowed on special occasions like weddings. Nevertheless both vocal and instrumental forms of music were cultivated, especially at the courts of the caliphs and princes and later by the Sufi orders.

ambivalence   am•BIV•uh•luhnts
(conflicting feeling toward a person or thing)
And there was an ambivalence about bees in the Scriptures. The Bible points out that while the bee's honey is a sweet nectar, its sting is a painful thorn.

ambulatory   AM•byuh•luh•taw•ree
(relating to the treatment and care of patients walking into and out of hospitals, clinics and doctors' offices.)
Deputy Mayor Ward argues that in the past, too much stress has been put on hospitals while facilities for ambulatory care and preventive services are substantially more effective.

amenable   uh•MEE•nuh•buhl
(submissive; responsive)
Not all Tibetans have been amenable to Chinese rule, and from 1959 until the early 1970's, the government presided over the destruction of more than 2,400 Lamaist monasteries.

amicable   AM•i•kuh•buhl
(friendly)
Treasury Secretary Blumenthal was another prime target, but his resignation was described as amicable and coming largely by mutual decision.

amorphous   uh•MAWR•fuhs
(without definite form; unorganized)
Since the independent truckers are a large and amorphous group of self-employed entrepreneurs, it is difficult to assess what their reaction will be to the latest call for a nationwide shutdown of their activities.

anachronism   uh•NAK•rah•niz•em
(anything that seems to be out of its proper time in history)

A reduction of tension would make it possible for the United States to phase out its military presence and put an end to what an official has called "the last of the cold war anachronisms in Asia."

anathema   uh•NA•thuh•muh
(a thing or person greatly detested)

To the conservatives in the Christian Democratic Party, he is anathema because he is a Socialist.

anecdote   AN•ik•dote
(a short, entertaining account of some happening)

But the best of his anecdotes makes the experience of the book worthwhile, especially if you happen to care about professional sports in America.

angst   angst
(a gloomy, often neurotic feeling of generalized anxiety and depression)

The assumption among theatre people is that word of a disaster in Boston is slow in reaching New York, while word of a disaster on West 44th Street, say, is around town in an instant. When this happens, there is depression, anxiety and general angst.

animosity   an•uh•MAHS•i•tee
(ill will)

Animosity sparked by the struggle—which centers on control of the community and the nature and direction of the resources that flow into it—has sent a current of tension through the neighborhood.

anomaly   uh•NAH•muh•lee
(a deviation from the common rule)

In an anomaly, gasoline consumption fell from June to July last year by about 350,000 barrels a day. Usually, use of gasoline remains steady or rises slightly in July.

antipathy
(strong dislike) — an·TIP·uh·thee

Many speakers voiced suspicion and antipathy toward science, reflecting the belief that technological "progress" has resulted in new forms of exploitation.

antiquated
(obsolete; out-of-date) — AN·ti·kway·tid

Yemen, on the other hand, has eight operational but antiquated MIG-15's and MIG-17's and the new squadron of American F-5E's for which there are no trained Yemeni pilots or ground crews.

antithesis
(exact opposite) — an·TITH·uh·sis

Yes, cheers for Slippery Rock, the school that to a lot of football followers symbolizes the antithesis of big-time college play.

apace
(swiftly) — uh·PACE

Iran's economic confusion also is growing apace.

apex
(peak) — AY·peks

Mr. McCoy's career reached its brief apex with "The Hustle," but it was hardly limited to that.

apocalyptic
(signifying imminent disaster and total or universal destruction) — uh·pah·kuh·LIP·tik

Hollywood's apocalyptic visions of mankind's doom have fingered locusts, grasshoppers, bees, Spanish moss, rabbits, frogs, sharks, worms, ants and carrots.

apolitical
(not concerned with politics) — ay·po·LIT·i·kuhl

The Baez songs (as they have been in her last few albums) are apolitical, while Miss Collins is so pop as to include two movie themes in her collection.

apprehensive
a•pree•HEN•siv
(anxious or fearful about the future)

Neither Oman nor Saudi Arabia, the two nations most openly apprehensive about the Soviet threat, want American troops on their soil, and American diplomats and military men agree.

arable
AR•uh•buhl
(suitable for producing crops)

President Anastasio Somoza Debayle owns one-tenth of all the arable land in Nicaragua, according to the agricultural advisers.

arbiter
AHR•bi•ter
(judge)

In any case, the public, which is the final arbiter, almost immediately makes up its own mind.

arbitrary
AHR•buh•trer•ee
(not going by rule or law)

Agonizing customs tie-ups and arbitrary rulings remain a major complaint.

arcane
ahr•KAYN
(understood by only a few)

In the arcane business of grain trading, the Kansas farmers could not be sure the Russians were placing orders for more wheat and corn. But somebody was, and their prices had risen above $4 a bushel by midweek, about 50 percent above last year's price.

archaic
ar•KAY•ik
(old-fashioned; antiquated)

Cable television systems already provide subscribers with news reports, stock market data and even shopping information, but these services seem almost archaic when compared with viewdata.

archetype   AR•ki•type
(a perfect example of a type or group)

Roedean has thus been able to remain what it has always been — an archetypal English girls' boarding school.

archipelago   ahr•kuh•PELL•uh•goh
(a group or chain of many islands)

Few outsiders follow the politics of this remote Indian Ocean archipelago, more than an hour's jet flight to the southwest from Colombo, the capital of Sri Lanka.

ardent   AHR•duhnt
(intensely enthusiastic or devoted)

Even her ardent supporters among lawyers and judges concede that Justice Bird can be quite abrasive.

arid   A•rid
(dry and barren)

Australian brush-tailed possums and bush rats, living in the desolate Western "outback" are waging a life-and-death contest with some succulent plants in their arid region.

Armageddon   ahr•muh•GE•duhn
(in the Bible, the place where the final battle between the forces of good and evil is to be fought before the Day of Judgment)

Is it Armageddon we are facing or just a miserable year or two?

articulate
(express clearly)   ahr•TI•kyuh•layt

The President acknowledged that he had become too bogged down in managing the Government and had not always spoken with a clear voice in articulating his goals and aspirations for the country.

artifact
         AHR•tuh•fakt
(any object made by human work; esp. a simple or primitive tool, weapon, vessel, etc.)

Archeologists rescued Egyptian and Eskimo artifacts at the American Museum of Natural History yesterday after a standpipe burst on the third floor.

ascetic
(self-denying)   uh•SET•ik

It had been my understanding that Michelangelo had led a fairly ascetic existence. I had read somewhere that his daily fare was generally bread and wine, which he ate and drank in solitude.

assail
(attack)   uh•SAYL

Attitudes toward the Cardinal shifted with time. Until mid-1964, he was esteemed by clergy and laity alike. But then he was assailed bitterly — even by some segments of the Catholic press — for his long silence on the racial question.

assertion
         uh•SER•shun
(a strong, positive statement)

Mr. Schlesinger and the Carter administration have generally accepted the assertion that the gasoline shortage is real.

assiduous
         uh•SI•joo•uhs
(done with constant and careful attention)

Arnold Guy Fraiman says he hates controversy, and for most of his life he has assiduously avoided it.

astronomic a•struh•NAH•mik
(extremely large)

A conservatory, yes, but a resident *opera?* "The costs are astronomic, it's not in the cards," Mr. Stevens says.

astute uh•STOOT
(clever or shrewd)

A harijan, or untouchable, he has served in every Indian Cabinet since 1946 and is regarded as an astute administrator.

asylum uh•SIGH•lum
(protection given by one country to refugees from another country)

The Soviet Union has asked Norway to return a 19-year-old soldier who walked across the border Monday and requested political asylum, the Foreign Ministry said today. He said he was "fed up with the Soviet Union."

atrium AY•tree•uhm
(a hall or entrance court)

My first full day back, my folks took me to see the new shopping atrium at the Citicorp headquarters.

audacity aw•DA•suh•tee
(daring; bold courage)

At first glance Maloney's decision to run his lightly raced filly against Davona Dale would appear to be the height of audacity.

audit AW•dit
(a formal examination and checking of accounts of financial records to verify their correctness)

In reporting on the utility's profit, an audit released yesterday also confirmed that Muny Light still owes Cleveland Electric Illuminating Company $5.1 million for electricity that it bought in the early and mid-

1970's. The audit was prepared by the accounting firm of Arthur Anderson and Company.

augment   awg•MENT
(increase)

They said the high-level proposal was likely to result in a gradual but significant augmentation of American naval and air forces in the region during the coming year.

august   aw•GUST
(imposing and magnificent)

Not many enclosed spaces in New York City are as august as the Blumenthal Patio in the Metropolitan Museum. It has at every season a grand, open, untrammeled look, and the open gallery that runs round two of its four sides at second-floor level is ideal for prints and drawings.

auspicious   aw•SPI•shuhs
(with signs of success; favorable)

NBC-TV's new newsmagazine series, "Prime Time Sunday," with Tom Snyder as host, made an auspicious debut in the national A.C. Nielson audience-popularity ratings.

authoritarian   ah•thor•eh•TAIR•ee•en
(exercising complete or almost complete control over the personal freedom of others)

While the South Korean economy booms, its political system remains rutted in authoritarian rule.

autonomy   aw•TAH•nuh•mee
(self-government)

Mr. Sadat defended Egypt's peace treaty with Israel and said his country would continue to negotiate with Israel and the United States to lay a foundation for Palestinian autonomy in the West Bank and the Gaza Strip.

aversion
(intense dislike)   a•VER•zhuhn

It started with the young man's aversion to studying and his theft of stationery from his classmates.

avert
(prevent)   uh•VERT

The theory now is that, with proper maintenance and repeated inspections, a repetition of the Chicago tragedy can be averted.

avid
(eager and enthusiastic)   AV•id

Apart from music, Mr. Fiedler was known best as an avid amateur fireman, and in 1970 he noted that he had been made an honorary fireman in 270 cities: "I've never left a concert to go to a fire, but I have left fires to go to a concert."

avocation
(pastime; hobby)   a•vuh•KAY•shuhn

As an avocation, he took up painting and, finding that little was known technically about the materials artists use, he set about assembling a reliable body of information on the craft side of painting.

awe
(a mixed feeling of reverence, fear and wonder)   aw

Displaying no respect and absolutely no awe for the team that is atop the National League West, the East's cellar-dwelling Mets struck early at Shea Stadium yesterday and shut out the Houston Astros, 4-0.

axiom
(a statement accepted as true; maxim)   AK•si•uhm

There is a baseball axiom that says games played early in the season are as important as games played in September. Earl Weaver, the manager of the Baltimore Orioles, is a believer.

B

badger — BAJ•er
(to keep on teasing or annoying)
McEnroe had been expected to be a favorite of the crowd, but quickly lost sympathy during the week. He badgered officials, complained about two penalty points awarded his opponents, and made snide comments about spectators who moved from their seats while he played.

balk — BAWK
(hesitate)
The fuel shortage has played havoc with store traffic, and customers are balking at menu prices that have been raised as many as six times this year to absorb higher beef prices and wage increases.

balmy — BAHM•ee
(mild)
Security measures were perhaps the strictest ever in this peaceful resort town, whose balmy climate makes it popular as a spot for wealthy Americans to retire.

bane — BAYN
(cause of distress)
For women in the suburbs, two things have long been their bane: waiting in lines — at supermarkets, at banks — and acting as chauffeur for the family.

BANE

banter BAN•tir
(playful, good-natured teasing)
In the Cub clubhouse, after chapel services, other players exchanged pregame banter as a radio blared with a male rock vocalist wailing, "I can't stand it no more, every woman made a fool of me."

bastion BAS•chen
(stronghold)
Perhaps the biggest factor is that in what seems an increasingly unsettled world the United States is regarded as the last bastion of free enterprise, a place hospitable to private property where claims will be honored by business and government.

bearish BARE•ish
(pessimistic)
He is notably more bearish about the future of Kennedy Center than Mr. Feinstein.

bedevil bi•DEV•il
(tormented)
Politically, he is bedeviled by the undeclared and unsettling challenge of Senator Edward M. Kennedy, whose tantalizing indecision about the 1980 Presidential race has kept the White House off balance.

beguile bi•GHILE
(charming or delightful)
Mary Pickford was the Peter Pan of the movies, with a face so fresh and innocent, so beguiling, that she could play child parts into her 30's, making audiences believe in her utterly.

behest bi•HEST
(earnest request)
Word was withheld at the behest of the police, who feared for the lives of the kidnapping victims.

belabor
(to spend too much time and effort on)
bi•LAY•ber

Miss Noska, who changed costumes for each of her three appearances, is the kind of performer who belabors everything with hamminess.

beleaguer
(encircle, as by an attacking force)
bi•LEE•ger

One of the ways devised to get mail out of the beleaguered city was the "Boule de Moulins," hollowed metal balls with vanes to be floated down the Seine River.

belittle
(to cause to seem unimportant)
bi•LIT•el

After the incident the coach frequently "benched" her, verbally belittled her and subjected her to other psychological harm.

belligerent
(hostile; quarrelsome)
beh•LIJ•ehr•ent

Last Monday the volatile Knight was reprimanded by the International Basketball Association for his belligerent behavior toward a referee and subsequent ejection during a victory over the Virgin Islands.

berate
(scold severely)
bi•RATE

Some coaches verbally berate a player in front of teammates and the press with the idea that it is a motivational technique that will improve future performance.

beset
(surrounded)
bi•SET

The parade's undisputed star, however, was the grand marshal, Eric Estrada, co-star of television's "CHiPs" who was beset by screaming, crying teen-age girls along the entire route.

bête noire   BET•nwar
(object of dislike)

Serge Koussevitzky, music director from 1924 to 1949, was Mr. Fiedler's particular bête noire.

bibliophile   BIB•lee•oh•file
(a person who loves books, especially for their style of binding, printing, etc.)

The DeKalb library branch began booming with young bibliophiles.

biennial   buy•EN•ee•al
(happening every two years)

The international aviation and aerospace community converged in Paris this weekend in the biennial bid for sales known as the Paris Air Show.

bilateral   BUY•lat•ehr•el
(affecting both sides equally; reciprocal)

Among the alternatives discussed at the White House meeting, officials said, was the establishment of a "special" bilateral arrangement with Saudi Arabia that would guarantee the United States long-term oil supplies at a fixed price.

bistro   BEES•troh
(a small nightclub)

This is Mr. Adler's first bistro stint here in four years.

bland   BLAND
(unexciting; uninspiring)

If the Yankees start to win under Martin, it will be agreed that he lent fire to a team that had grown apathetic under a bland manager.

blatant   BLAYT•ent
(outrightly obvious)

"It's so blatantly restrictive of the right of assembly and free speech that it's a joke."

bleak   BLEEK
(not promising or hopeful)

But even if the civilians do take over on schedule, Ghana's immediate future appears bleak.

blithe   BLYTH
(showing a cheerful, carefree disposition)

That's James Bond, who, by all rights, should be an antique, as emblematic of the 60's as the Beatles and flowerpower, but who goes blithely on as if time has had a stop.

blitz   BLITS
(bombardment)

Listening hint: Starting at 3 P.M. on Sunday, WKCR-FM will offer a Miles Davis blitz, lasting 125 hours, including everything he ever recorded.

BLITZ

bolster
(support)   BOWL•ster

The Anchorage Times, dominant in the market since it was founded a half-century ago, has begun printing a midday edition to bolster its street sales.

boon
(blessing)   BOON

There are some precooked foods, however, that are an absolute boon to anyone who has menu-planning and cooking by the kitchen clock in mind, and one of them is sliced boiled or baked ham.

boondocks
(a remote rural area)   BOON•dox

Suffolk County, once considered the political boondocks, is likely to have three full Congressional districts — as many as Nassau and Manhattan and more than the Bronx.

boondoggle
(work of little or no practical value done merely so one is busy or looks busy; pointless work)   BOON•dog•el

To New York City it would be a boon; to the rest of the country it looks like a boondoggle.

bouillabaisse
(a chowder made with several kinds of fish and shellfish, vegetables, seasoning, etc.)   boo•yeh•BASE

"It's a fantastic fish. In Marseilles they don't throw it away, they throw it into the bouillabaisse," he responded.

bourgeoisie
(the middle class)   boorzh•wa•ZEE

Shortly after the State Legislature reluctantly appropriated $200,000 to buy the island in the Detroit River for park land in 1879, Detroit engaged Frederick Law Olmstead, the designer of Central and Prospect Parks, to remake the two-mile-long island into a park befitting the city's rising industrial bourgeoisie.

brashness
(pushiness; impudence)   BRASH•ness

Coming from Maloney, that kind of confidence can't be dismissed as brashness.

bravura
(display of daring)   breh•VYOOR•a

In a bravura of Mediterranean warmheartedness, Italy dispatched three naval ships to try to rescue 1,000 Vietnamese from the high seas off Malaysia.

brazen
(bold)   BRAY•zen

The midnight murderer had time to cut the man's wallet from the pocket of his trousers, hanging by the bed, and walk out of the house with the couple's top dresser drawer, brazenly pausing to rifle its contents a few blocks away.

breach
(to break through)   BREECH

Some fans got word of Martin's arrival and breached the security area at the airport where only those with tickets are permitted to enter.

brusque
(rough and abrupt in manner and speech)   BRUSK

Decades of success never entirely mellowed Mr. Shumlin, a Colorado rancher's son with a booming voice who could be as brusque as a drill sergeant.

bucolic
byoo•KOL•ik
(relating to country life; rustic)

A young man is attracted to a gypsy girl, and, as lovers do in bucolic ballets, they dance happily together.

bulwark
BULL•werk
(a strong defense or protection)

No other democracy has ventured so far in assuring access to the billions of secret documents that form one of the bulwarks of bureaucratic power.

buoy
BOO•ee
(to keep afloat; hold up)

The disaster brought a vast inflow of foreign aid and credit that buoyed the economy for several years.

burgeon
BUR•jen
(develop rapidly)

We wrote some weeks ago of a burgeoning fresh caviar business recently begun on the West Coast.

cache
KASH
(a hidden store of food or supplies)

Forty-four pounds of cocaine and a weapons cache of more than 40 firearms, including a machine gun and thousands of rounds of ammunition, were seized in raids Friday on three Queens apartments, drug-enforcement authorities said yesterday.

cachet ka•SHAY
(a distinguishing mark of quality)

The word today is "minimal." It used to be "understated." The meaning hasn't changed, however. Clothes that are simple, uncluttered and spare have an instantly recognizable cachet.

cacophony ka•KOF•ah•nee
(harsh, jarring sound)

"The Wolfman" consists of a cacophonous barrage of distorted electronic squawking on tape, fevered electric-keyboard effects and Mr. Ashley grimacing and moaning into a microphone, his sounds twisted by howling feedback.

cadence KADE•ence
(measured movement)

The Elis were handily beaten by the more experienced British squad, which never dropped its racing cadence below 40 strokes to the minute during the race.

cajole ka•JOLE
(coax with flattery)

An effort to cajole owners of tax-exempt real estate into making "voluntary payments" in lieu of property taxes has yielded many letters of explanation but few dollars.

callous KAL•es
(hardened and unfeeling)

Talk among the troopers, typical of war, was callous, peppered with references to "gooks" and "houts," racial epithets for the guerrillas.

camaraderie kam•eh•RAD•eh•ree
(frendliness and loyalty among comrades)

There were the usual complaints about food and insufficient rehearsal time, and a camaraderie born of tension in the dancers' dormitories.

candor
KAN•der
(honesty and openness of expression)
In a letter sent yesterday to the President, Mr. Ford said, "You have made a compelling assessment of the crisis in confidence that besets us, and I think the public will respond to your leadership and candor."

capitulate
kap•PICH•eh•late
(give in)
"The I.O.C. does not usually capitulate. We discuss and sometimes we compromise."

capstone
KAP•stone
(highest point)
President William R. Tolbert, Jr., the new chairman of the Organization of African Unity, has looked forward to the position he assumed this week as a capstone to his long political career.

carp
KARP
(to find fault)
Despite the carping of critics over the years, the Dow with its 30 component stocks has represented "the market" to millions of investors.

cartel
kar•TELL
(an association of industrialists, business firms, etc., for establishing a national or international monopoly by price fixing, ownership of controlling stock, etc.)
Asked how the West and Japan could "break the oil suppliers' cartel." Mr. Miyazawa said that the oil consumers must convince moderate members of OPEC, notably Saudi Arabia, that continued price increases were self-defeating and would undermine growth in the developed world.

cascade
kas•KADE
(a series of waterfalls)
It is highly improbable — but not impossible — that a

single lightning bolt this summer could start a cascade of mishaps and misjudgments that would black out almost the entire United States east of the Rockies.

castigate KAS•teh•gate
(scolding severely)

After castigating other writers for years for misusing "who" and "whom," Mr. Bernstein turned against "whom." He had a rubber stamp made so he could print on his correspondence, "I favor whom's doom except after a preposition."

cataclysm KAT•eh•kliz•em
(a great upheaval that causes sudden and violent changes)

Not everyone believes a social cataclysm lies ahead, but some observers do not rule it out.

catalyst KAT•eh•list
(a person or thing acting as the stimulus in bringing about or hastening a result)

After examining those women's programs which did receive grants, the Ford Foundation study stated, "A catalyst in many programs was the presence of a woman in a position of power who helped mobilize the effort."

cavalier kav•ah•LEER
(casual or indifferent toward matters of some importance)

His attitude at orchestral rehearsals could be deceptively cavalier — "a most tedious and unnecessary affair" he can be heard to remark during a taped session while going over a Haydn symphony in preparation for a recording.

censure SEN•sher
(a judgment or resolution condemning a person for misconduct)

Prime Minister Morarji R. Desai, faced with a censure

chafe   CHAFE
(to become irritated or impatient)
Rosen is not the first to chafe under Steinbrenner's controls.

chagrin   shah•GRIN
(a mixture of embarrassment and annoyance because of failure or disappointment)
With some chagrin, his chief of staff, Diane Coffey, who is in charge of car assignments, acknowledged yesterday, a year and a half into the Koch administration, that the New York City's car fleet had not been cut at all.

charisma   ke•RIZ•mah
(a special quality of leadership that captures the popular imagination and inspires allegiance and devotion)
There was also a feeling expressed by some liberals that charismatic leadership of the kind associated with the Kennedys was no longer the answer to the nation's troubles.

charlatan   SHAR•le•ten
(a fake)
"Consequently you are, so to speak, nothing but a mangy charlatan who pretends to cure the mange of others while his own remains incurable."

chary   CHAR•ee
1. *(not giving freely)*
She was generally chary of radio appearances except as a guest expert on "Information Please," and she was little seen on television.

2. (on one's guard; cautious)
Be prepared also, if you hunt a specific area several days in a row, for a fish that showed little or no fear the first time around to become chary of your approach.

chasm KAZ•em
(a deep gap)
He was influenced by Dr. Alva Taylor, a socialist, whose concept of the "social gospel" helped him formulate his stand against the chasms between the rich and the poor and the treatment accorded blacks.

chaste CHAYST
(free of sexual content; pure)
Though made in 1979, "Moonraker" is as chaste as a '50's film; when one pretty girl is about to die, the camera pans to the trees overhead, and when another pretty girl is about to be seduced, the camera pans to the moon above.

CHASTE

chastise chas•TIZE
(scold)
One woman reporter was chastised about the length of her short skirt before Mr. Roloff finally ordered the press off his property altogether.

chauvinist SHO•va•nist
(unreasoning, militant and boastful devotion to one's country)

The company has also shed its chauvinist image — Ei ji Toyoda once said he would never invest in the United States, where workers are sloppy and undisciplined. And the Toyota board has canceled a motion passed a decade ago never to admit a foreigner.

cherub CHER•eb
(a person, esp. a child, with a sweet, chubby, innocent face)

A short, baldish man with blue eyes and a cherubic face, Mr. Slade did his best work under pressure, but in off hours, friends recalled yesterday, he was an amiable raconteur who loved to play poker with other reporters and photographers.

chic SHEEK
(fashionable)

Terrorism, Michael Selzer says, has become chic.

chide CHIDE
(to scold mildly)

Publicly, Republican leaders have refrained from criticizing the President while he has formulated his program, except to chide him for not including more Republicans in his meetings.

chutzpah HOOT•spa*
(a Yiddish word meaning "nerviness," audacity or gall)

But, as I realized while watching Al Pacino's production of "Richard III," there is a kind of theatrical daring, a quality of *chutzpah*, about Mr. Shakespeare that a number of our tamer dramatists might do more than envy. They might try having a whack at it.

* hoot as in foot

circumscribe SER•kum•skribe
(to restrict)

There are several vibrant, highly literate church weeklies and monthlies, though their circulation is carefully circumscribed and they are heavily censored.

circumvent ser•kum•VENT
(to go around or bypass)

Eager to circumvent currency restrictions and send money abroad, Iranians are buying quantities of prized Persian rugs, shipping them overseas as exports and depositing the earnings in foreign banks.

cite SITE
(to refer to or mention by way of example)

Citing a jogger he saw running backwards and sideways, Mr. Orechio said: "That's the kind of lunatics we have pursuing the sport of jogging."

clandestine klan•DES•ten
(secret)

Levi Strauss's presence in Moscow may also give a boost to its hopes of eventually making jeans and casual clothes in the Soviet Union for a market reportedly so jeans-mad that Levi Strauss's jeans sell there for $150 a pair — when they can be clandestinely obtained from visitors.

clangor KLAN•ger
(a clanging sound)

From somewhere behind locked steel doors and four-foot thick concrete walls comes the faint clangor of an alarm bell.

cliché klee•SHAY
(an idea that has become trite)

When you serve the bread, an attractive vessel is a straw basket the same shape as the loaf and lined with a checkered napkin. That's a cliché in a restaurant, but I think it is a warm thing to do at home.

coalition   koh•ah•LISH•un
(a temporary alliance for some specific purpose)
Taxi fares are scheduled to go up 15 cents a ride at 6 A.M. today, but a coalition of independent cab owners has vowed not to charge the increase, protesting that it is not high enough.

coerce   ko•ERSE
(to force or compel to do something)
HEADLINE: Califano Cites Feuds and Politics; Blumenthal Denies Being Coerced.

cohorts   KO•horts
(associates)
The British press had surprisingly few editorials about the reorganization, but several papers have taken the occasion to write unflatteringly about Mr. Carter's Georgia cohorts.

collusion   kah•LOO•zhen
(a secret agreement for fraudulent or illegal purposes)
They asked if United States oil corporations are in collusion with OPEC.

commensurate   kah•MEN•sher•it
(proportionate)
The spokesman said the United States had also urged

Vietnam to reduce the flow of refugees to a rate "commensurate with the international community's ability to care for them."

commiserate   ke•MIZ•eh•rate
(to sympathize)
"Was that the right way to do it?" asked an aide whose job was not likely to be affected but who commiserated with her colleagues. "Is there a right way to fire people? I don't know," she replied, shaking her head. "I don't know."

commodious   kah•MODE•ee•us
(roomy)
Home at sea is a commodious 15-foot-square stateroom that Lieutenant Edwards shares with Ens. Eleanor Hotton, a biology graduate from the University of Colorado.

communiqué   ke•MYU•neh•kay
(an official communication or bulletin)
Following are excerpts from the text of a communiqué issued today by President Carter and President Park Chung Hee of South Korea at the end of Mr. Carter's two-day visit here:

complacent   kom•PLAY•sent
(self-satisfied)
Jim Spencer said that nothing about the Yankees surprised him any more — "I've seen it all" — but he disagreed with the suggestion that the team had become complacent. "There are too many guys here on the last year of their contract," Spencer said. "Anybody with future aspirations isn't going to be complacent."

complement   KOM•pleh•ment
(complete or bring to perfection)
One of the most interesting salads we've made re-

cently combined cubed boiled ham with cut-up endive, two foods which, cold or hot, complement each other.

complicity   kom•PLISS•et•ee
(involvement in wrongdoing)

Walter Knop, 66 years old, was sentenced today to nine years in prison for complicity in the murder of 159 prisoners from the Gassen concentration camp in February, 1945.

composure   kom•PO•zher
(calmness of mind or manner)

With all the verbal bullets flying, Mr. Schlesinger retains his public composure. But there are hints that he is frustrated for want of a national energy policy.

conciliatory   kon•SIL•yeh•tor•ee
(seeking to win over or to overcome distrust or hostility)

Swept into office by a coalition of conservatives, Dr. Rogers today sounded conciliatory toward all 13.1 million Southern Baptists.

concurrent   con•KUR•ent
(occurring at the same time)

The jury then recommended that Mr. Henly, 23 years old, serve six concurrent life terms in prison.

condescending   kon•di•SEND•ing
(behaving as though one is superior)

At some of the masses the Pope celebrated in Warsaw and Czestochowa, sophisticated blue-jeaned youths of the cities chuckled condescendingly at the elderly peasants who arrived from the countryside in the colorful regalia of the past.

condone   kuhn•DOHN
(to forgive, pardon or overlook)

Noting that Mr. Connally did not even mention the

environmental consequences of stepping up coal production and nuclear power, Tom Tatum, an energy spokesman said, "We cannot condone the rape of American land and water. Energy conservation remains the cornerstone of Administration policy."

conducive   kon•DOO•siv
(helpful)
That industry will increasingly be expected to provide an atmosphere conducive to the health of workers was one of many themes to emerge in a study on "Lifestyles/Personal Health Care in Different Occupations."

conduit   KON•doo•it
(a passageway for conveying wires, cables and other equipment, rather than people)
After breaking through the wall and crawling along a maze of pipes and conduits, they emerged from the building through a hole in the wall of a 60-cell wing under construction.

configuration   kon•fig•yeh•RAY•shun
(shape; outline)
She is loaded with computers and complex electronic gear that can pinpoint her position on the globe within a few hundred yards and discern configurations not much bigger than a breadbox on the ocean floor several miles below.

confluence   KON•floo•ents
(a flowing together of two streams)
The confluence of the summer tourist season, the opera season and, beginning today, the summit season, has strained the facilities of this old imperial capital to the limit.

congenital   kon•JEN•eh•tel
(inborn)
Dick Buerkle was even farther behind in 4:17.9, both-

ered by a congenital breathing deficiency that left him with the equivalent of a 4:38 mile and vowing never to return.

conjecture   kon•JEK•cher
(guesswork)

How soon after that he could unveil an energy plan remained a matter of conjecture.

conjunction   kon•JUNK•shun
(joining together; union)

What brought about this conjunction of international artists in a New York suburb?

connoisseur   kon•eh•SIR
(a person who is especially competent to pass critical judgments, especially in the arts or in matters of taste)

To a connoisseur of German wines, the names of these vineyards, perched on the dizzying slopes overlooking the Rhine, are almost sacred.

connotation   kon•eh•TAY•shun
(an idea associated with a word in addition to its explicit meaning)

"Behavior modification has gotten a bad connotation because most people think of surgery and drugs when you mention it," said Richard Brightman, an instructor. "All we mean by the term is rewarding the child with praise, hugs, or a favorite toy for each small step he makes in learning."

consensus   kon•SEN•ses
(agreement)

Members of the Organization of Petroleum Exporting Countries reached a consensus tonight that there will be a split oil price on world markets, then adjourned their meeting for the night.

consortium   kon•SORE•she•em
(a temporary alliance of two or more business firms in a common venture)

New York City officials announced yesterday that a consortium of 40 city, out-of-state and foreign banks had agreed to serve as a "backup" lender for $600 million in short-term notes that the city will market publicly in the next five months.

consternation   kon•ster•NAY•shun
(great fear that makes one feel helpless or bewildered)

Scores of such incidents, together with the outcries over Three Mile Island, have created an atmosphere of consternation over the hazards of radiation and led to a polarization of public opinion.

constraint   con•STRAYNT
(restriction)

However, Mr. Stone thought that topical humor might run into constraints even on public television.

contemporary   kon•TEM•peh•rer•ee
(concerning the present time)

Although he described writing as an avocation, he produced scholarly books with sharp, probing investigations into contemporary problems.

contention   kon•TEN•shun
(a statement that one argues is true)

It is his contention, and I am inclined to agree, that fine restaurants will willingly cook foods without salt by request.

contentious   kon•TEN•shuss
(tending toward disputes; quarrelsome)

The British economy hasn't changed all that much in three years. There is still high inflation, a contentious work force and the lowest level of productivity growth in the West.

contiguous   kon•TIG•yoo•us
(next to; touching)

German vineyards are rarely contiguous with the home or the winery of the man who makes the wine.

contingency   kon•TIN•jen•see
(an unforeseen or accidental occurrence)

There are also contingency plans under which Laker, if the grounding went on for months, could lease planes from other carriers.

contingent   kon•TIN•jent
(a group forming part of a larger group)

There were television cameras, a large contingent of reporters and a larger than usual crowd at Rutgers Stadium.

conventional   kon•VEN•shen•el
(in accordance with tradition)

While conventional versions of Charles Dickens' "A Christmas Carol" are playing on home television screens next December, a new, unconventional version—set to jazz and gospel music — will be playing on Broadway.

convivial   kon•VIV•e•yel
(friendly and festive)

Both areas have a convivial street life that attracts the young and provides ready traffic for eating places that are informal and moderately priced.

co-opt
ko•opt

(to persuade or lure an opponent to one's own system, party, etc.)

One curious thing is that President Carter could have made it harder for Senator Kennedy to be a challenger by co-opting him, but he has not. For example, the Administration went ahead lately with a medical program different from Kennedy's though the Senator thought the differences could have been compromised quite readily. If they had been, Senator Kennedy would have been tied up as the Administration's pointman on that issue.

cosmetic
koz•MET•ik

(concerning the improvement, change or beautification of only the surface)

Treaty advocates had hoped that he might merely seek mild and "cosmetic" modifications of the treaty and support it on the final vote.

coterie
KOTE•eh•ree

(a close circle of friends who share a common interest or background; clique)

Mr. Califano is said to have offended many in the department by relying mostly on a small coterie of bright young assistants.

counterculture
KOWNT•er•kul•chur

(the culture of many young people of the 1960's and 1970's manifested by a life style that is opposed to the prevailing culture)

Mr. Ruffin traces the current interest in preventive health and alternative therapies to the counterculture of the 60's.

counterpart
KOWNT•er•part

(a person or thing closely resembling another)

But the indomitable New Yorkers of 1829, like their 20th-century counterparts, refused to let the rain spoil Independence Day.

coup KOO
(short for "coup d'état," a sudden, forceful stroke in politics, esp. the sudden, forcible overthrow of a government)

The latest coup, in which at least 13 persons were killed, was the fourth in Ghana's 22-year history as an independent nation, but the first in which any lives were lost.

couturier koo•TUR•ee•eh
(a designer of women's fashions, esp. one in the business of making and selling the clothes he or she has designed)

Long before the days when photographers lit up the runways with their strobes and their flashes, a couturier's fame was spread by the glamour of his customers.

covert KO•vert
(secret)

A covert attack could be made by a single terrorist able to penetrate an airfield or a missile site, destroy the complicated security apparatus and hold the nuclear weapons "hostage."

covet KUV•et
(to desire eagerly)

To most of the high-ranking women in the space industry here, the most coveted job is that of astronaut.

cower COW•er
(to crouch or huddle up in fear)

The wounded Miss Johnson was picked up quickly by four men led by Sgt. David Firth, a 34-year-old veteran of the British Army in Ireland, who found her cowering beneath a bush.

craven KRAY•ven
(very cowardly)

Hadn't the Finns, in craven self-censorship, refused to publish Solzhenitsyn?

credence KREE•dence
(believability)
The general gave credence to President Assad's statement that he would not be dragged into battle at a place and time he did not want.

creditable KRED•it•eh•bull
(deserving credit or praise)
Although he allowed the third Minnesota goal, he did creditable work in his first league appearance here this season.

criterion kreye•TEER•ee•on
(a standard of judgment)
In both the Halperin and Smith cases, the appeals court said, there appeared to be no evidence that a national security threat was involved—the criterion for wiretapping without a judge's warrant.

crocodile tears KROK•eh•dial
(insincere tears or a hypocritical show of grief: from an old belief that crocodiles shed tears while eating their prey)
OPEC shed crocodile tears for the poor developing countries hit by higher oil prices, promising them $800 million in new aid, enough to buy 40 million barrels at the new price.

cronyism KRO•nee•izm
(favoritism shown to close friends, esp. in political appointments)
They are unabashed practitioners of cronyism—bringing old friends and classmates into senior jobs.

culinary KYOO•leh•ner•ee
(relating to cooking or the kitchen)

There are, by the way, a variety of "grinds" of black pepper and, theoretically, each serves a different culinary purpose.

cull   KUHL
(to examine carefully so as to select or reject)
She used to cull the mail and save the nastiest for him. He enjoyed answering them personally.

culminate   KULL•mih•nate
(to bring to a climax)
The sale culminates almost three years of hearings, studies and court battles between environmentalists, oil companies and Government agencies.

cumbersome   KUM•burr•sum
(hard to handle because of size, weight, etc.)
It is the Brooklyn Philharmonia CETA Orchestra of New York, whose cumbersome title now has been officially reduced to Orchestra of New York.

curator   KYOO•rate•er
(a person in charge of a museum, library, etc.)
Mr. Houghton is a former curator of rare books at the Library of Congress and a former trustee of the New York Public Library.

cursory   KURS•eh•ree
(hastily done; superficial)
Mr. Sheldon limits his very cursory descriptions to physical details, and on those rare occasions when his characters do any thinking, they think out loud.

curtail   kur•TALE
(to cut short; reduce)
Gas purchases in the New York area also usually peak on weekends during the summer and service stations faced with shortfalls curtailed their weekend hours first, exacerbating the weekend lines and probably causing a panic.

dearth
DIRTH
(scarcity)
Adolfo's fans will be rustling in taffeta next fall. Stavropoulos followers will, as usual, be floating in chiffon. Either way, there will obviously be no dearth of romantic, decorative evening dresses.

debacle
day•BAH•kuhl
(a stunning, ruinous collapse or failure)
Ironically, Lorillard was an important client of Lennen and Newell, the ad agency, whose failure in 1972 was the worst financial debacle in advertising history.

debilitate
di•BILL•eh•tate
(weakening)
As a result of this inactivity and a debilitating bout with infectious hepatitis, Mr. Aalto "would get tired carrying a bag of groceries home."

decadence
DEK•eh•dense
(deterioration and decay)
Ayatollah Khomeini in a speech also published today urged religious leaders to campaign for the Islamic republic and combat "Western" corruption and decadence.

decapitate
di•KAP•eh•tate
(to cut off the head)
There are any number of reasons to cook a fish whole: It looks so much grander, for one thing, than when it's decapitated and bereft of its tail.

decelerate dee•SELL•eh•rate
(slow down)
Carter Administration officials who had been expecting the fast-rising prices to decelerate as the year progressed are now expressing second thoughts.

decipher dee•SIGH•fer
(to make out the meaning of)
There were some markings on the gauze-like wrappings around the mummy, which the scientists have not been able to decipher.

decisive dee•SIGH•siv
(settling without further question)
The longstanding proposal to substitute direct popular election of the President for the Electoral College was defeated decisively in the Senate today and appeared to be dead for the foreseeable future.

déclassée day•kla•SAY
(having lost class)
"It is no longer considered déclassée to be seen at a bus stop," said a Malibu resident who no longer drives the 70 miles round trip to downtown Los Angeles.

decorum di•KOR•um
(proper behavior)
Representative Jim Mattox sought to deal with the heat by showing up on the floor without a coat or tie, an almost unimaginable sartorial slight to two centuries of Congressional decorum.

de facto di•FAK•to
(existing as such, although without lawful authority)
On his return here at the age of 20, he was promoted to major and, by the time his father was assassinated in 1956, he was a full colonel and de facto leader of the National Guard.

defect   di•FEKT
(to desert a cause, country, etc., esp. in order to adopt another)
Miss Strachonova is the second major woman tennis star to defect from Czechoslovakia. Martina Navratilova, the Wimbledon champion the last two years, defected to the United States four years ago.

dejected   di•JEKT•ed
(in low spirits; depressed; disheartened)
Watson, who came into this tournament as the heavy favorite, was dejected and tired after his round.

deleterious   del•eh•TEER•ee•us
(injurious to health)
Nevertheless, on Aug. 10, 1958, the United Nations Scientific Committee on the Effects of Atomic Radiation concluded: "Even the smallest amounts of radiation are liable to cause deleterious genetic, and perhaps also somatic, effects."

deletion   di•LEE•shun
(to take out a printed letter, word, etc.)
Minutes before the deadline for a 9 P.M. newscast, Mr. Lapid forced editors to make some deletions.

delude   de•LOOD
(deceive)
However, the argument goes, the Soviet Union does not delude itself into thinking it can throw the United States out of Africa or any other zone of American interest, and has no wish to let this form of rivalry get out of hand.

deluge   DEL•yooj
(flood)
Mr. Seiler said that he had been deluged with offers from all over the world for a piece of Skylab—ranging from $20,000 from the West Australian Museum to a

caller from Hong Kong who promised an ounce of gold for every ounce of Skylab that was found.

demagogue DEM•eh•gog
(a person who gains power and popularity by arousing the emotions, passions and prejudices of the people)

Mr. Koch added, "We are very lucky with Andrew Stein because a smart demagogue can be very dangerous, but Andrew is not dangerous."

demean di•MEEN
(to lower in dignity or standing)

"This conduct demeans me, demeans our profession and demeans my office," the justice said. "The hostility is such that I must tell the commission that I will be unable to answer Mr. Delizonna's questions."

demeanor di•MEE•ner
(outward behavior)

Despite a cheerful demeanor, Mrs. King, six-times singles champion here, said: "I'm ticked. I hate to lose."

demise di•MIZE
(end of existence)

The energy crisis brought about the demise today of the decades-old requirement that male reporters wear coats and neckties in the House press gallery.

demure di•MYOOR
(shy and modest)

The female flies to within four inches of the male, hangs in front of him and demurely lowers her wings as a signal, whereupon the male presents his gift.

denigrate DEN•eh•grate
(speak damagingly of)

There probably isn't an executive in all of television who would denigrate — at least in public — the value of electronic journalism.

denouement day•NOO•mah
(the outcome, solution, unraveling or clarification of a plot in a drama, story, film, etc.)

Mr. Wilder is well aware that the denouement of "Fedora," the unraveling of the dreadful secret, comes midway through the film.

denounce di•NOWNCE
(condemn openly or publicly)

More than 20,000 people who poured into an open field today heard the Diablo Canyon nuclear power plant denounced by folk singers, nuclear power opponents and the Governor of California.

deplete di•PLEET
(to decrease seriously)

If there was a major concern for New York, it involved a depleted pitching staff that is still without Ron Guidry, Goose Gossage and Jim Beattie.

deploy dee•PLOY
(to place strategically)

Mr. Brezhnev wants to continue the negotiating process on strategic arms into the 1980's to include missiles deployed in Europe, which are not covered by the new treaty.

depose di•POZE
(remove or oust from office)

Idi Amin, the deposed President of Uganda, is living in exile in Libya, United States officials said today.

deprecating DEP•ri•kate•ing
(expressing disapproval; to belittle)

As the characters go through their stock routines — Talia Shire shyly whispering "I love you," Mr. Stallone making self-deprecating jokes, Burgess Meredith telling the kid he's either a bum or a hero — you get the feeling that you've been here before. Well, you have.

derelict   DER•eh•likt
(a destitute person, without a home or regular job and rejected by society)

They said a derelict who had been sleeping in one building injured an elbow when he jumped from a second-floor window to escape the flames.

deride   di•RIDE
(ridicule)

At a time when it's fashionable to deride the social welfare experiments of the 1960's, the food stamp program has survived and flourished.

de rigueur   deh•ree•GER
(strictly required, as by etiquette, usage or fashion)

Slips, for instance, are no longer *de rigueur*. Neither are girdles.

derivative   di•RIV•eh•tiv
(unoriginal; derived from someone else's concept or style)

In 1954, he was a gifted but derivative singer and guitarist; by the time he began recording at Petty's studio in February 1957, he was an original.

despondent   di•SPON•dent
(depressed; dispirited)

Parents naturally become concerned when they see their children despondent and miserable because of an athletic experience.

desultory   DESS•ull•tor•ee
(aimless; random)

When we first arrived at Lobsterville Beach on Martha's Vineyard, I cast my lure in desultory fashion because there were no signs of striped bass or baitfish close to shore.

détente
day•TAHNT
(a relaxing, esp. of international tension)
Soviet society has been exposed to more American influence during this decade of détente than in any other period since the Bolshevik Revolution, deepening the ambivalence that Russians have historically felt toward the West.

detractor
di•TRAKT•or
(one who disparages the reputation or worth of something)
According to offical figures, 40 were killed. But other reports put the number of dead in the hundreds, and the Government's detractors referred to the event as the Tlatelolco massacre.

detrimental
deh•tri•MEN•tul
(harmful)
Caution: working may be detrimental to your health.

DETRIMENTAL

devastate
DEV•eh•state
(to lay waste; ravage; destroy)
Just the effect of human visitors and their dune buggies can be devastating to the desert. The thin layer of desert soil is protected from erosion by a fine crust composed of fungi, algae and mosses. When this crust is broken by a wheel or foot, the soil can easily erode, bringing an end to the desert's ability to support life.

devotee
(enthusiast; fan)   dev•eh•TEE

Siluetas metalicas, a game that entails shooting with highpowered rifles at steel silhouettes of animals, came into the United States from Mexico in the 1960's, and now it is attracting thousands of new devotees each year.

diabolical
(devilish)   die•eh•BOL•i•kul

A marvelously diabolical trap suddenly decided the otherwise level game between Grandmaster Wolfgang Unzicker and a master named Dankert in the 14th round of the Munich International Tournament.

diaphanous
(so sheer and light as to be almost transparent)   die•AF•eh•ness

Miss Green was resplendent in a diaphanous blue and purple outfit, speckled with gold, that offered a goodly glimpse of what lay underneath, something frowned upon in China.

diatribe
(a bitter, sharply abusive criticism)   DIE•uh•tribe

During her demonstrations Mrs. Rorer would offer a lengthy diatribe against eating one thing or another, all the while preparing that very dish.

dichotomy
(division into two parts)   die•KOT•uh•mee

"It's a real dichotomy: you have to be very tough and unemotional and professional to deal with the business part, but then when you get the job you have to let the toughness go to get the vulnerable, open part of yourself."

dictum
(an authoritative pronouncement)   DIK•tem

Neckties are no longer at half-mast, in keeping with Mr. Carter's dictum to his staff to cinch up or ship out.

diffidence DIF•eh•dence
(timidity; shyness)

I am described for example, as dancing with Miss Nin, a pleasure I distinctly remember denying myself out of diffidence.

diminutive deh•MIN•yoo•tiv
(small)

"Hollerin'," interjected Georgia Oliver, his wife, a diminutive, sunny woman with ranks of sun-tanned laughlines marching away from her china-blue eyes. "Hollerin' is an art."

dire DI•er
(indicating trouble; threatening)

Dire predictions that a nationwide food shortage could develop this week proved to be far from true, despite a continuing strike by independent truckers.

discern di•SURN
(make out clearly)

Out at the observable edge of the universe, we can faintly discern fascinating objects as they were when they sent us their light more than 15 billion years ago.

discombobulate diss•kum•BOB•yoo•late
(upset the composure of; confuse)

You'll recognize Mr. Smith's name more easily as the front end of Smith and Dale, the vaudeville comedy team that introduced the discombobulated Dr. Kronkite to the world.

disconcert diss•kon• SERT
(to disturb the self-possession of; perturb)

The model I have is made of orange plastic, which I find disconcerting. It gives me the feeling that I must have acquired this thing in some toy department.

disconsolate .   diss•KON•so•let
(hopelessly unhappy; inconsolable)
Discouraged at the referee's decision to stop the fight, Shuler stalked annoyingly about the ring and left disconsolate after accepting his silver medal.

discord   DISS•kord
(conflict; lack of harmony)
Scientists and theologians today ended a two-week World Council of Churches conference with a plea for a common effort to overcome discord between their two fields and to embark together on a broad search for truth.

discreet   dis•KREET
(careful about what one says or does)
Mr. Lockwood is known — if he's known at all — to patrons of Lincoln Center in general and the Mostly Mozart Festivals in particular as a tall, graciously self-possessed man who comes forward after intermissions and makes discreet, remarkably inoffensive pitches for money.

discrepancy   dis•KREP•en•see
(lack of agreement; inconsistency)
Officials also sought to clear up the time discrepancies surrounding the delay in reporting the fire.

disenchanted   dis•en•CHANT•ed
(losing belief in one's illusions)
Asserting that Democrats and Republicans were sidestepping the major economic and social issues facing the United States, a group of disenchanted activists, most of them liberals, today announced the formation of a Citizens Party that would field its own Presidential candidate in 1980.

disgorge   dis•GORJ
(to pour forth)

A new record is almost certain to be set this year for the amount of oil disgorged into the seas through spills, blowouts and tanker collisions.

disgruntled   dis•GRUNT•tulled
(grumblingly discontented)

Mr. Thien Quang said the various religious groups had formed secret communication links and were organizing disgruntled Vietnamese for an uprising in 1981.

disparate   DIS•pahr•it
(widely different)

She was, it appeared, a devoted member of such disparate organizations as the Animal Medical Center and the National Conference of Christians and Jews.

dispel   dis•PELL
(cause to vanish; disperse)

And by simply being friendly to the people, the Sandinists have swiftly dispelled the fear and tension that long gripped Managua.

disquieting   dis•KWIGH•uh•ting
(disturbing; upsetting)

During the unfolding of the scandal, other disquieting news came out of North Carolina.

disseminate   diss•EM•eh•nate
(to spread widely)

The National Rifle Association — 1600 Rhode Island Avenue N.W., Washington, D.C. 20036 — disseminates information on rules and regulations for rifle and pistol silhouette shoots.

dissertation   diss•er•TAY•shun
(a formal and lengthy essay written by a candidate for a Ph.D. thesis)

His dissertation, to be completed by August, is a social and economic study of the city of Aleppo, Syria, in the 18th century.

dissident
DISS•eh•dent
(an outspoken critic of a government or other ruling body)

The South Korean Government announced today the release of 86 dissidents, most of them university students, and said more would be freed if they promised not to engage in anti-Government activities.

dissociated
diss•OH•she•ate•ed
(severed, as though one had never been a part of)

"He is dissociated from his past, and he wants to make sense out of his life."

distraught
diss•TRAWT
(extremely troubled; deeply agitated)

Alicia de Larrocha, the Spanish pianist, is distraught over the loss of a small suitcase that was not there when she picked up the rest of her luggage at the Philadelphia airport July 21 after her Aerolineas Argentinas flight from Buenos Aires.

docile
DOSS•ell
(easily managed or handled)

"It's not that we have great power," said Mr. Anraku. "It takes enormous effort to persuade people to fall in line. The Japanese are not as docile as foreigners think."

doldrums
DOLE•drums
(a state of inactivity)

Tourism, which could be Tanzania's most vital source of income, is beginning to make a comeback after years in the doldrums.

doleful
DOLE•full
(sorrowful; mournful; melancholy)

Two-thirds of the fish consumed is imported, which, Richard Frank observes, has some doleful implications.

dormant DOR•mant
(as if asleep)

The 27-year-old Lynn has not been dormant until now. There was the 1975 season, "when no rookie did what I did." He set a rookie mark of 47 doubles, hit .331, scored 103 runs and drove home 105.

dote DOTE
(to bestow excessive fondness)

At 67, Mrs. Ratia is a major figure in Finland. Like many countries, this one dotes on its athletes, but unlike most, it also dotes on its designers.

dotty DOT•ee
(feeble-minded)

The plot involved an aging young man's frantic efforts to get rid of his elderly, dotty mother.

dynasty DIE•neh•stee
(the period during which a certain family reigns)

With the end of the 46-year-old Somoza family dynasty apparently only days away, few Nicaraguans were yet aware that the President might be willing to step down.

earthy UR•thee
(simple and natural; hearty)

The food served here is definitely homestyle, making up in earthy goodness what it lacks in finesse.

ebullient   eh•BULL•yent
(overflowing with enthusiasm; high spirited)
Much to the discomfort of Communist and Vatican officials, here was a man of relaxed good humor who was going to say essentially what he thought; an ebullient figure, laughing, weeping and announcing that reading prepared texts was a bit of a bore and that ad libbing was much more fun.

ecclesiastical   ih•klee•zee•AS•ti•kull
(pertaining to the church or the clergy)
Invoking a rarely used provision of ecclesiastical law, the Roman Catholic Archdiocese of New York refused yesterday to allow a funeral mass to be offered for Carmine Galante, the reputed underworld leader slain last week.

echelon   ESH•uh•lon
(rank)
These people are from all echelons of society, but the backbone of the church is working-class people, who provide heavy financial support for their churches even as they struggle to make ends meet.

eclectic   eh•KLEK•tik
(composed of material gathered from various sources)
The music is an eclectic mixture of blues, ballads, calypso, and rock, with even a few bars of boogie-woogie.

ecosystem   EK•oh•sis•tem
(a system formed by the interaction of a community of organisms with their environment)
Over-exploitation by man could radically alter the entire Antarctic marine ecosystem.

ecumenical   ek•yuh•MEN•ih•kull
(promoting better understanding among different religious faiths)

This ecumenical service was part of a serious attempt by two major religious groups to create a ceremony for Christians and Jews who wish to worship together.

effervescence   ef•ur•VES•ense
(bubbliness)

There was, of course, the ubiquitous Eubie Blake, still, at the age of 96, talking, playing piano and singing with undiminished effervescence.

effusive   i•FYOO•siv
(overly demonstrative)

Mr. Wahlman said he was thanked effusively and was told, "You'll hear from us soon."

elated   ih•LATE•ed
(in high spirits; joyful)

He said that United was elated with the success of the half-fare coupons.

elicit   ih•LISS•ut
(to draw forth)

The President had gone out of his way at the outset of his Administration to elicit specific pledges from each of his Cabinet selections that they would remain a full four years.

emaciated   ih•MAY•she•ate•ed
(abnormally lean, as from starvation or disease)

They found the child's emaciated body lying on a couch and summoned an ambulance.

embellish   im•BELL•ish
(to decorate or improve by adding ornaments; adorn)

"I've got clothes from the last 10 years in there, so I don't plan to buy any clothes this summer. I'll take my basic wardrobe and embellish it with new accessories: belts or pins or scarves."

embroil   im•BROYL
(to involve in trouble)

Mr. Jordan has periodically become embroiled in social mishaps. At one time, a woman he met in a bar contended that he spat a drink at her, and the White House felt compelled to issue a long brief in his defense.

emigrate   EM•eh•grate
(to leave one country to settle in another, the opposite of "immigrate," which means to enter a new country after leaving another)

Mr. Esiner survived the ghetto and several Nazi concentration camps and emigrated to the United States after the war, becoming a millionaire textile manufacturer.

empirical   im•PIER•ih•kel
(derived from experience or experiment, rather than from theory or faith)

Among the 450 participants are scientists from most of the major fields of empirical study and theologians from a wide spectrum of churches.

emulate   EM•yuh•late
(to imitate with an effort to equal)

The French government announced today a wide-ranging energy conservation program that will be presented at the upcoming economic summit meeting in Tokyo as a model for other nations to emulate.

encroach   in•KROACH
(intrude)

Limiting speeds would be "substantial encroachment on personal liberty," said Dionys Jobst, a member of Parliament from Bavaria.

endemic   en•DEM•ik
(constantly present in a particular locality)

Mr. Ladd's initial announcement startled the film and investment communities and was thought to underscore an endemic problem plaguing major movie studios: how to keep essentially creative executives happy in essentially administrative roles.

endowment   in•DOW•ment
(a bequest or gift that provides an income for an institution or person)
Mr. Rodgers has done more than write music for the theatre. He has also provided a million-dollar endowment to help finance productions in New York of new musicals by authors not yet recognized in the professional theatre.

enigma   ih•NIG•muh
(a puzzling occurrence or situation)
HEADLINE: Energy Policy: An Enigma Surrounded By a Riddle.

enmesh   en•MESH
(entangle)
"It is too early for black people to become enmeshed in speculation on who to support or who to run in formal primaries in the black community."

ennui   on•WE
(boredom)
Spectators at the Board of Estimate's seven-hour session at City Hall yesterday showed signs of ennui during the slow-moving proceedings.

ensconce   en•SKONCE
(settle securely and comfortably)
Ensconced in his bunker, General Somoza is described by aides as being in a somber mood.

ensemble   on•SAHM•bull
(a small group of musicians playing or singing together)

Stephen Simon, music director of the County Symphony, noted a few days ago that his ensemble is no longer made up of musicians from Westchester.

entourage   on•too•ROZH
(attendants, as for a person of rank)
By nightfall some of Ali's old entourage had gathered — Drew (Bundini) Brown, Gene Kilroy and Wali Muhammad.

entrench   en•TRENCH
(securely establish)
American officials are aware of the fragile state of Mr. Brezhnev's health, but they believe that he is still solidly entrenched at the top of the Soviet leadership and remains the man to talk to despite infirmities.

entrepreneur   on•truh•preh•NOOR
(a person who organizes and manages a business, usually with considerable initiative and risk)
Entrepreneurs, cash in hand, have been meeting incoming passengers to try to buy the half-fare coupons.

environs   in•VIE•ronz
(surrounding area; vicinity)
Make no mistake about it: Richard Nixon is looking forward to returning to New York City or its environs this autumn and to pursuing a more visibly active life.

envisage   en•VIZ•ij
(to picture; imagine)
"The prestige of the President is becoming lower and lower, and therefore it is very hard to envisage his re-election."

equation   ih•KWAY•zhun
(association)
Most Americans who supported the peace movement during the Indochina war were not proponents of a

equestrian ih•KWES•tree•en
(on horseback)

A mile away, cheering crowds pulled down an equestrian statue of the deposed President's father, Gen. Anastasio Somoza Garcia, who founded the Somoza family dynasty more than four decades ago.

Communist victory, even though the Johnson administration — and particularly the Nixon Administration — tried hard to make that equation.

equestrian ih•KWES•tree•en
(on horseback)

A mile away, cheering crowds pulled down an equestrian statue of the deposed President's father, Gen. Anastasio Somoza Garcia, who founded the Somoza family dynasty more than four decades ago.

equitable EK•wit•eh•bull
(fair; just)

Advocates argue that this plan would be most equitable as it would not discriminate among people according to their wealth.

erratic i•RAT•ik
(in no fixed pattern)

Dripping with sweat, everybody tumbled off into the chaos of the waiting room, where it was announced that all remaining shuttle flights had been canceled because of erratic and severe thunderstorms along the East Coast.

erroneous eh•ROH•nee•es
(wrong)

Eugene Gold, the Brooklyn District Attorney, called the report "wild hypothesis unsupported by any evidence." A spokesman for the New York City police said the report "appears to us to be erroneous."

ersatz ER•zats
(artificial; synthetic)

Mr. Brownlow presents a keen glimpse of the process that turned the real West into the movies' West almost overnight, leading to the creation of ersatz cowpokes like Tom Mix, who is examined here in particularly amusing detail.

erstwhile   URST•wile
(former)

Garry Davis, the erstwhile "world citizen" who renounced his American citizenship in 1948 to dramatize his belief in world government, is finally trying to come home.

eschew   es•CHOO
(to shun; avoid)

The artist wrestles with his guilt and makes himself whole. In this fashion, he taps the true fountain of morality, and reaffirms man's capacity to choose good and eschew evil.

esoteric   es•uh•TER•ik
(understood by or meant for only the select few who have special knowledge or interest)

The energy crisis has opened up some unusual job opportunities, and perhaps none is more esoteric and more fruitful than the field of palynology, the study of pollens.

esthetic   es•THET•ik
(pertaining to beauty)

Speaking of matters esthetic in the subways, it now seems clear that the program of station-painting inaugurated with much fanfare earlier this year — and praised in this column — has not had quite the positive effect that was expected.

estranged   es•TRAINJD
(turned from an affectionate or friendly attitude to an indifferent, unfriendly or hostile one)

Although estranged from her rock star husband, Mick Jagger, she remains a "jet set" personality and, as such, dutifully visited refuge centers and made vague offers of help to the local Red Cross.

estuary ESS•choo•were•ee
(the mouth of a river, where the tide meets the current)

Those who want to spear fish in the estuaries should check the state's laws to find out where, legally, salt water ends and fresh water begins.

euphemism YOO•feh•miz•em
(a mild or inoffensive word substituted for one that is more direct or blunt)

With inspiration worthy of the Pentagon, NASA wordsmiths have devised the jolly euphemism "Skylab's footprint" for the as yet unlocated target area.

euphoria yoo•FOR•ee•uh
(a feeling of well-being or high spirits)

Only a short time ago, all divisiveness was seemingly swept away by the euphoria of the Israel-Egypt peace treaty.

exacerbate ig•ZASS•er•bait
(intensify)

The leader of Libya, Col. Muammar el-Qaddafi, was reported yesterday to have decided to halt exports of crude oil for at least two years. The news sent tremors through world financial markets, stirring fears that such a step would increase oil shortages and exacerbate inflation.

excise ek•SIZE
(cut out)

The documents and tapes are filled with classified national security information and highly personal items about Mr. Nixon and his family. Before they are released, if they ever are, the documents are to be carefully reviewed to excise these portions.

excoriate ek•SKOR•ee•ate
(denounce harshly)

The design of the building is still excoriated, the very concept of a large-scale, multi-purpose cultural center is dismissed as corrupt or unworkable, and the size of both the budget and the bureaucracy required to run it is regarded as a folly.

exhaustive ig•ZAW•stiv
(covering every possible detail; thorough)

Dr. Williams, who won the 1970 Pulitzer Prize for an exhaustive biography of Huey Long of Louisiana, was 70 years old.

exhort ig•ZORT
(to urge, advise or caution earnestly)

Pravda exhorted its readers, "Let every person who produces fuel or uses electrical or fuel energy ask himself: has he done everything to raise production and avoid waste at the production level?"

exhume ig•ZYOOM
(dig up)

Because the United States took so long to develop concert music identifiable as distinctly American, we do not have centuries of repertory to exhume and examine.

EXHUME

exodus EK•seh•dus
(a departure of a large group of people)

Hanoi strongly denied responsibility today for the exodus of hundreds of thousands of refugees from Vietnam, Laos and Cambodia and placed all blame on the United States and China.

exonerate ig•ZON•uh•rate
(to free from blame)

"The neurotic person," said the late Karen Horney, "insists on his guilt and vigorously resists every attempt to exonerate him."

expedite EK•spuh•dite
(to speed up the progress of; hasten)

The virgin gas fields in Alaska await only the building of a pipeline, which President Carter has pledged to expedite.

explicit ik•SPLISS•it
(clearly stated, and leaving nothing implied)

It was a balmy Friday in early June when the 50-word memo was distributed without fanfare in the White House press room. What it said had been said before, but never quite so explicitly: "The Secretary of the Treasury is the Administration's chief economic spokesman."

exploitation ek•sploy•TAY•shun
(the unethical use of something or someone for one's own advantage or profit)

"I met 49 of the finest girls in America at the Miss America Pageant," she said. "It's not true that it's used for sexual exploitation. The bathing suit appearance is 10 minutes out of a two-hour program."

exponent ik•SPO•nent
(representative)

Jay McShann, a jazz pianist and singer who is an exponent of Kansas City-style blues, will begin a four-week engagement at Michael's Pub, 211 East 55th Street, next Tuesday.

expound   ik•SPOUND
(set forth)

The West is still a safe haven for Russians who think differently, a place from which they can expound views that filter back into the rarefied atmosphere of the Soviet intelligentsia.

expropriate   eks•PRO•pree•ate
(to take from its owner, esp. for public use)

The Asbestos Corporation lost another round in court today in its battle to prevent the possible expropriation of its assets by the Quebec government.

expunge   ik•SPUNJ
(to erase or remove completely)

In another report, Norman Cousins, chairman of the board of the Saturday Review, warns against reliance on a single strategy to expunge illiteracy.

extol   ek•STOLE
(to praise highly)

HEADLINE: Entertaining: A Chef Extols The Virtues of Simplicity

extortion   ik•STOR•shun
(the act of getting money through threats, misuse of authority, etc.)

HEADLINE: Closed Hearing Denied Convicted Extortionist

extradite   EK•struh•dite
(to turn over an alleged criminal or fugitive to another nation or authority)

Paraguay is coming under increasing pressure to apprehend and extradite Dr. Josef Mengele, a Nazi concentration camp physician who escaped to Latin America after the war, officials here say.

extraterrestrial   ek•stra•tuh•RES•tree•ull
(originating outside the limits of the earth)
Another writer says he was visited by extraterrestrial beings at his home in the forest.

extremist   ik•STREEM•ist
(a supporter of extreme doctrines or practices)
"But every time you say this, you are labeled as an extremist — you are labeled as someone who is trying to destroy industrial world growth."

extricate   EK•struh•kate
(to set free; disentangle)
Temporarily at least, many politicians believe that the President's seminars at Camp David have extricated him from the political embarrassment of last week's canceled energy speech.

fabrication   fab•rih•KAY•shun
(falsehood)
"This energy scare is a total fabrication. There is no scarcity; there is only the psychology of scarcity."

facade   fuh•SOD
1. (the front of a building)

The restaurant's indented brick facade is framed by small yellow lights.

2. (a superficial appearance or illusion of something)
The critics regard the Muzorewa Government as a facade for continued white control in Zimbabwe.

facetious   fuh•SEE•shuss
(not meant to be taken seriously or literally)
Some traditionalists believe that the quarterback is being coddled, thus compromising the form of this contact sport. It has been facetiously suggested that quarterbacks play inside shark cages.

facilitate   fuh•SILL•uh•tate
(to make easier)
A small glass plate, trademarked as the Cain Encoder, promises to facilitate the automatic reading of electric and gas meters.

faction   FAK•shen
(clique)
If the broad alliance opposed to the Somozas breaks up into political factions fighting for power, the outlook will be even grimmer.

factitious   fak•TISH•ess
(artificial; contrived)
Records are made to be broken — even such factitious ones as "highest price paid at auction for a modern painting." The new champion is Henri Matisse's "Le Jeune Martin I" ("The Young Sailor") purchased last week by an anonymous buyer at London's auction house of Christie, Manson & Woods for $1,576,800.

fait accompli   fay•ta•kom•PLEE
(a thing already done, so that opposition or argument is useless)
During the three weeks before the deals were an-

nounced, rumors about them were aired by TV and radio stations in Nashville. But both Nashville dailies blacked the story out until it was a fait accompli.

fallacy   FAL•uh•see
(a false or mistaken idea)
"Don't ever embrace the fallacy that brandy makes mince pie more digestible. Never. It preserves the mince in your stomach exactly as it preserves in a bottle."

falter   FAWL•ter
(to lose strength; weaken)
Mr. Rogers, who is 36, has made a career of taking over faltering grocery operations in Cleveland's black neighborhoods and putting them on their feet.

fastidious   fas•TID•ee•us
(hard to please; excessively critical or demanding)
"The Japanese are fastidious, their culture makes them want to change cosmetics with every season and they like beautiful packaging," Mr. Rogers explained.

fatuous   FA•chew•us
(foolish)
Perhaps it sounds fatuous to object to heavy miking for disco music, but this is part of the fundamental contradiction between disco and theatre.

feisty   FIE•stee
(energetic; spirited; full of fight)
Harry S. Truman, the feisty President, once advised those who could not stand heat to get out of the kitchen.

ferret   FER•et
(to search out or bring to light)
The agency is sending a specially equipped helicopter to ferret out spots showing the most radiation.

fervid FER•vid
(enthusiastic)

Mr. Forsyth is a British entertainer who apparently has a large and fervid following on stage and on television in his home country.

fetid FET•id
(having an offensive odor; stinking)

The settlements were even more fetid before international groups such as the Salvation Army began arriving last month. Now conditions are improving.

fiat FEE•at
(order; decree; esp. when arbitrarily introduced by a person or group of persons having absolute authority to enforce it)

The lesson in all this seems to be that the political currents of contemporary Latin societies cannot be reversed by military fiat.

fiefdom FEEF•dom
(a hereditarily held piece of land, ruled by a lord and inhabited by his subjects)

Over the years, secured in power by unswerving loyalty to Washington, the Somoza family was able to turn Nicaragua into its personal fiefdom, growing enormously rich while smothering all opposition in the name of fighting Communism.

finagle fuh•NAY•gel
(to get or achieve something by cleverness, trickery or deception)

The last coupon-bearing flights will take off Sunday night, but both airlines said that finagling for coupons would go on, although in a different form.

fin-de-siecle fan•du•SYEKL
(end-of-the-19th century)

A fascinating, fin-de-siecle figure, Schreker wrote

music that luxuriates opulently somewhere between Mahler and Berg.

finesse — fuh•NESS
(skill)
Andy Bean, exhibiting the power and finesse that has established him as one of professional golf's young stars, shot an 11-under-par 61 and took a five-stroke lead today after three rounds of the $300,000 Atlanta Classic.

fiscal — FISS•kuhl
(financial)
Motivated by fiscal considerations, Truman placed a $14.4 billion ceiling in 1950 on the defense budget.

flagrant — FLAY•grent
(outrageously noticeable)
Reggie Jackson was suspended for five days on July 19 for flagrantly disregarding the manager's instructions while at bat.

flamboyant — flam•BOY•unt
(showy)
Mr. Shumlin was a striking figure, even among other flamboyant theatre-district figures, because he shaved his head daily — and began doing so, his friends said, well before head-shaving was given a certain currency by Otto Preminger and Yul Brynner.

flaunt — FLAWNT
(to parade or display conspicuously or boldly)
Jimmy Connors flaunted tasseled socks one day that shook up and down as he dove for cross-court passing shots.

flux — FLUKS
(continuous change)
As a result, nude beaches are in constant flux, toler-

ated and on the rise in some communities, scorned and on the run in others.

foment   fo•MENT
(stir up; instigate; incite)

The Prime Minister also used his speech to denounce Marxist guerrillas, accusing them of fomenting trouble among the Kurds, Arabs and other ethnic minorities.

forbears   FOR•bares
(ancestors)

"We four take pride in having rediscovered a social pattern that was second nature to our frontier forbears," Mr. French said.

forbidding   fur•BID•ing
(threatening; disagreeable; grim)

The underlying tax issue, though cloaked in forbidding terminology and technical details, is reasonably clear-cut.

forgo   for•GO
(to give up; do without. Not to be confused with "forego," which means "to go before; precede," although it is sometimes spelled that way, too)

He attended Exeter and, then, forgoing a scholarship to Yale, returned to Detroit to audition for Jessie Bonstelle's drama school.

forlorn   for•LORN
(dreary; abandoned)

Saks and several other fine stores are still here but others have been replaced by cheaper shops that give the otherwise gracious street a forlorn air.

formidable   FOR•meh•deh•bull
(strikingly impressive)

The big work on the program was Brahms' Sonata in F minor, and it called forth the afternoon's most formidable performance—serious, honest and cleanly and accurately articulated.

forte FOR•tay
(a thing at which one excels; strong point)
"My forte is taking a contemporary theme—widowhood, mother-daughter relationships, interracial marriage, et cetera—and building around it."

founder FOWN•der
(break down; collapse)
Innumerable attempts have been made to reconcile the two regimes, only to founder on the implacable hostility and suspicion that have built up over the 26 years since the Korean War.

fracas FRAY•kus
(a noisy fight or loud quarrel; brawl)
More than 100 persons were arrested yesterday, and 24 were injured as the eight-hour fracas spread along a 70-mile stretch of farmland between Watsonville and King City.

fractious FRAK•shes
(hard to manage; irritable)
A weary and fractious New Jersey State Assembly in the early hours today debated a controversial plan to create a state transportation authority that could buy and run railroads and buses.

fragile FRAJ•el
(delicate; easily damaged)
"There's one sight I'll never forget," he said. "As I stood on the Sea of Tranquillity and looked up at the earth, my impression was of the importance of that small, fragile, remote blue planet."

fraternize FRAT•ur•nize
(to associate socially)

No fraternization between the 200 women inmates and the men is allowed.

frayed FRAYD
(worn; ragged)
They reach the airport just in time for their plane, at a cost of severely frayed nerves plus $23 for the cab, including a tip for the driver.

FRAYED

free-wheeling free•WEEL•ing
(not governed or influenced by rules)
A cookery expert translated Mrs. Whistler's free-wheeling instructions ("take a handful of flour") into more precise measurements.

frivolity fri•VOL•eh•tee
(light-mindedness; of little importance)
It is one of the tenets of male chauvinism that shopping is a frivolous female activity, but perhaps the male personality might benefit from a touch of frivolity.

fruition froo•ISH•un
(a coming to fulfillment)
"I feel I have fulfilled my destiny. What I've done these last few years is the essence of my whole life. I've brought it to fruition."

fruitless FROOT•less
(unsuccessful; vain)
Mr. Hightower and his wife, who are black, were attracted to the neighborhood seven years ago after fruitlessly looking in the suburbs and on Staten Island for a home in an area where they would feel comfortable.

funk FUNK
(an earthy, blues-based quality characteristic of some modern music, particularly jazz)
Commercial funk musicians like George Clinton or Bootsy Collins would undoubtedly recognize some of the bass and drum patterns in Mr. Ulmer's music, but more commercial funk is tightly organized and single-mindedly dance-oriented.

fusillade FYOO•suh•lade
(a simultaneous or continuous discharge of firearms)
They survived the fusillade by three gunmen and fled from the Joe and Mary Italian-American Restaurant at 205 Knickerbocker Avenue in the Bushwick section.

galvanize GAL•vuh•nize
(to stimulate as if by an electric shock)
Mrs. Sharp said that what galvanized her into action in an effort to get the book published was a visit to the Pentagon with other wives of Congressmen.

gamut   GAM•ut
(the entire range or extent)

The magazine has also prepared a number of retirement guides and sells a kit of them along with subscriptions. They cover the whole gamut of retirement interests, including money.

garrulous   GAR•uh•luss
(excessively talkative, esp. about unimportant things)

"The Talkative Suitor": The title sums up the plot—a garrulous young man wins his bride from objecting parents on the condition that he stop his incessant talking.

gastronomy   gas•TRON•eh•me
(the art or science of good eating)

Although Mrs. Rorer occupied an enviable position in the annals of American gastronomy, the last years of her life were pathetic.

gaunt   GAWNT
(thin and bony; hollow-eyed and haggard)

Gaunt from weight loss, bearded, disheveled and with gray hair falling well below his shoulders, Mr. Niehous "looked like a middle-aged hippie," according to a reporter who saw the six-foot-one-inch businessman leaving a military helicopter after his rescue Saturday.

gauntlet   GAWNT•let
(a former military punishment in which the offender had to run between two rows of men who struck him with clubs, etc. as he passed)

By 10 o'clock, with the sun high in the sky, stifling heat, clouds of gnats around my face and an occasional horsefly bite, each cornrow was a torture gauntlet.

genteel   jen•TEEL
(belonging or suited to polite society)

Because of the colonial experience of these countries,

getting bronzed was not considered genteel because it was associated with outdoor labor. As a result, suntan lotion was not heavily promoted.

germane   jer•MANE
(relevant; pertinent)
The judge directed Pullman to show Mr. Berry's lawyers those portions of the report that Pullman's lawyers contended were germane to the settlement of Mrs. Wolfson's suit.

gestation   jes•TAY•shun
(pregnancy; period of development)
There are many ways of putting together a Broadway show, although the usual one involves anxiety, talent and a gestation period of, say, two years.

glower   GLAU•er
(a sullen look; scowl)
Out on the Yankee Stadium scoreboard, Thurmon Munson's face looked down from the huge screen, his walrus mustache dominating his familiar glower.

glut   GLUT
(excessive supply)
This feast of sports on television is a treat for viewers and cable operators, but for the people who run the professional sports leagues and those who own franchises, and even some of the athletes, the glut of sports in the living room is a cause for concern.

goad   GODE
(prod into action; incite)
So he takes out newspaper ads trying to goad Rocky into a rematch.

gracious   GRAY•shuss
(pleasant and courteous; hospitable)
"Socially, he is one of the most generous men I have ever known, gracious and thoughtful."

grandiose   GRAN•dee•ose
(having grandeur or magnificence)

The entire production is dominated by the superbly inventive and grandiose score of Hans Werner Henze.

graphic   GRAF•ik
(vivid)

(7) Movie: "The Desert Rats" (1953). Richard Burton, James Mason, Robert Newton. Graphic but lacks impact. (1 hr. 50 mins.)

grass roots   GRASS ROOTS
(the common or ordinary people, as contrasted to the leadership of a political party, organization, etc.)

Beneath the facade of calm in Crown Heights is a grass roots struggle for power among activists on both sides.

gratis   GRAT•iss
(free of charge)

At dinner, fresh fruit is served gratis.

gratuity   gruh•TOO•eh•tee
(money, over and above payment due for service; a tip)

"We kindly suggest that a gratuity may be left for courteous and efficient service."

gravitate   GRAV•i•tate
(to have a natural tendency or be strongly attracted)

Female runners and male runners should not gravitate

to one another in one corner of the room, laughing privately at dirty running jokes and freezing out outsiders.

gregarious   greh•GARE•ee•us
(fond of the company of others; sociable)
William M. Ellinghaus, A.T.&T.'s gregarious president, said: "I think the Bell System has a great future."

grievous   GREE•vus
(severe)
By the time ground troops reached the scene the most grievously wounded woman was dead.

grimace   GRIM•us
(a twisting or distortion of the face)
The second set was tied, 6-6, with the tiebreaker at 5-3, with Vilas leading, when the 24-year-old Pecci fell on the court, grimacing and pointing to the calf of his left leg.

grouse   GROWSE
(to complain; grumble)
At one point, he said, she groused about her life in New York: "Sure, there is good theatre and opera, but as I don't go out in the evenings, what good is it to me? I might as well be living on a desert island."

habitué   huh•BICH•oo•way
(a person who frequents a particular place)

Discothèque habitués know the routine best. They sleep mostly in the evening and set alarms for the wee hours when the action at the discos gets going. Motorists in Medford, L.I., have now joined the reverse sleeping pattern too.

hackneyed   HAK•need
(made commonplace or trite)
The forms he uses may be familiar, even hackneyed, but in this instance, at least, the sculptor understands what it takes for a work to survive in a busy urban setting.

halcyon   HAL•see•un
(calm; peaceful; happy; idyllic)
Although these targets are somewhat ambitious, they were met during the halcyon year of 1974.

harbor   HAR•ber
(to hold in the mind; cling to)
All the while he harbored deep in his heart the conviction that the country really did need a publication that "humanized the crazy world of art and was written by people who could write."

harried   HA•reed
(harassed)
"You wouldn't believe this place," said one harried secretary. "This is a public information office, and people have been calling in cursing, complaining and threatening us."

harrowing HA•roh•ing
(keenly or painfully disturbing)
(9) Movie: "The Ox-Bow Incident" (1943). Henry Fonda, Dana Andrews, Anthony Quinn, Jane Darwell, Strong, harrowing drama of Western lynching. One of the best. (1 ½ hrs.)

haute cuisine OAT kwih•zeen
(fine, skillfully prepared food)
Tante Claire sometimes goes in for the sort of over-complicated dishes that the English confuse with haute cuisine, and a recent visit proved that keeping it simple should be a major dictum of eating out in London.

haven HAY•ven
(a safe place; refuge)
The tragedy of the Vietnamese "boat people" denied havens and turned back to sea has evoked painful memories of the suffering of Jewish refugees from Nazi Germany and has sparked a demand by Jewish and Christian agencies for immediate and extensive governmental assistance.

havoc HAV•uk
(great destruction and devastation)
The threat that the disintegrating space station could rain havoc over a wide area had captured attention around the world in recent weeks as space agency controllers tried to predict and control when and where it would fall.

hedonism HEED•en•iz•um
(the self-indulgent pursuit of pleasure as a way of life)
However, this group is deeply entrenched in hedonism, and has thus far turned a deaf ear to the needs of the country.

heinous HAY•nus
(outrageously evil or wicked)

Theodore R. Bundy was sentenced today to die in Florida's electric chair by a judge who called the 1978 slayings of two college sorority sisters "indeed heinous, vicious and cruel."

herculean   her•kyuh•LEE•en
(requiring the strength of a Hercules)
Even if the tactic works, Mr. Golob said, managing the oil that has already escaped is a herculean task.

hermetic   hur•MET•ik
(completely sealed; airtight)
The good news is that, after centuries of hermetic isolation, the government here has decided to allow two or three tourists a day to come to Lhasa.

hiatus   hi•ATE•us
(a break or interruption in the continuity of something)
Americans were permitted to own gold bullion beginning in January 1975 after a 40-year hiatus.

hierarchy   HIGH•uh•rahr•kee
(any system of persons or things ranked one above the other)
Today, at age 79, Mr. Chen is perhaps the second most influential man in the Communist hierarchy, ranking in real terms only after Deng Xiaoping, the senior Deputy Prime Minister.

high-handed   hi-HAN•ded
(overbearing)
He was incensed, he said, at what he termed the high-handed way the United States has treated Mexico, which has large oil reserves.

hinterlands   HINT•er•landz
(the remote or less developed parts of an area)
Private commuter bus lines serve the urban hinter-

lands, rumbling into suburbs and outlying districts where public systems can't, or won't, tread.

hitherto HITH•uhr•too
(until now)

This year he is embarking on a venture with Fila, an Italian company hitherto noted for its tennis and swim wear. Fila is going into golf clothing, with Watson and Nancy Lopez as the principal models.

Holocaust HOL•uh•kost
(When the initial letter is capitalized, this word refers to the systematic destruction of over 6 million European Jews by the Nazis before and during World War II. When the initial letter is lower case, the word denotes a great or total destruction of life, esp. by fire)

"For years I have been struggling to reconcile myself with the Holocaust, and I decided that I would never be able to understand the cruelty," said Mrs. Lantos, who lectures on the Holocaust.

homily HOM•uh•lee
(a sermon)

In his homily he repeated the call to Christian courage that has been the theme of his nine-day visit to Poland.

honorarium on•uh•RARE•ee•um
(a payment to a professional person for services on which no fee is set)

The honorarium for the clergyman is the bridegroom's obligation.

horde HAWRD
(a mass or crowd; swarm)

A horde of some 2,400 journalists from more than 25 countries has converged here in the last few days, snapping up every available bed and rental car.

hybrid HIGH•brid
(the offspring of two distinct types or species)

The chance mating of two species of ape in an Atlanta zoo has led to the birth of a healthy offspring — the first reported ape hybrid.

hypothetical hi•puh•THET•ih•kel
(theoretical; supposed)

No one knows the answer to such questions, but a number of factors have made the questions real and not hypothetical.

I

icon I•kon
(in the Orthodox Eastern Church, an image or picture of Jesus, Mary, a saint, etc., venerated as sacred)

All told, there are 12 monasteries in Cyprus, all decorated with Byzantine icons.

iconoclast igh•KAH•nuh•klast
(one who breaks with the traditional, often ridiculing the cherished beliefs of others)

Mr. Ladd is reputed to have an iconoclastic bent and an uncanny eye for commercial properties. It was Mr. Ladd, for example, who decided to make George Lucas's "Star Wars" after several other studios turned the project down.

idiom ID•ee•um
(characterstic style)

Grover Washington can play his saxophones, and he seems to have a genuine feeling for the jazz-funk idiom.

imbroglio   im•BROL•yo
(an involved and confusing situation)

But try as it might, Pullman finds itself still caught up in the passenger-car business, and the company is now at the center of an imbroglio over subway cars it sold to New York City.

imminent   IM•uh•nent
(about to happen; impending)

There have been rumors about Look's imminent demise for some months as the magazine has gone through a succession of editorial changes.

impasse   IM•pass
(a standstill in affairs; deadlock)

The impasse was broken late yesterday when high Tanzanian officials said that they recognized Mr. Binaisa and not Mr. Lule as President.

impassive   im•PASS•iv
(not feeling or showing emotion)

Since the trial began a week ago, all three defendants had listened impassively to the testimony until yesterday's incident.

impeccably   im•PE•kuh•blee
(faultlessly)

Mr. Hamilton sat in the perpetual twilight of the bar of the Regency Hotel, facing the piano player, gazing into his scotch and soda, impeccably turned out always in a gray doublebreasted suit, striped shirt and polkadot tie, deeply tanned, not a hair out of place in that helmet of glossy black, now edged with gray.

impede   im•PEED
(to bar or hinder the progress of; delay)

Reporting about the election, which began on Saturday and is to continue on weekends through Aug. 11, has been impeded by the Nigerian Government's refusing entry to some news organizations, including The New York Times.

impending   im•PEND•ing
(about to happen; threatening)

This is why you should get out of or off the water and put down your fishing rod and golf clubs at the first sign of an impending thunderstorm.

imperative   im•PER•at•iv
(absolutely necessary)

It is imperative that the Government initiate a full-scale investigation, coupled with public hearings, into the operations of the nation's oil companies.

imperious   im•PEER•ee•us
(domineering; overbearing)

And on the day before he died, when he was visited in his hospital room by his wife, Diana, and by the playwright Howard Teichmann and his wife, Evelyn, Mr. Shumlin imperiously told his visitors exactly where to place themselves around the room.

impetus   IM•pet•us
(anything that stimulates activity; driving force or motive)

Dr. Denmark said the impetus for her research had come from a woman instructor's complaint that she had been denied promotion because she spoke her mind at faculty meetings.

impinge im•PINJ
(to touch; have an effect)
And, simply put, energy and inflation impinge on virtually every household in the country, while arms control remains a far more abstract and intangible issue.

implacable im•PLAK•uh•buhl
(that cannot be appeased or pacified)
The implacable and irreconcilable enemies of the arms limitation treaty intend to vote for outright rejection. But first they plan to offer so-called "killer amendments," designed to alter the accord so extensively that the Soviet Union will refuse to ratify it.

implement IM•pluh•ment
(to carry into effect)
Implementation of his order would involve, among other changes, the busing of more white students.

implicit im•PLI•sit
(suggested or understood without being plainly expressed; implied)
Implicit in the ending of "Moonchildren" was the notion that somewhere, around the next corner after college, there was an apparently stupid life to be got through.

implore im•PLORE
(to ask or beg earnestly for)
Protesting truckers, men and women, have blocked diesel pumps with their rigs and are imploring other truckers, with mild curses, not to buy fuel.

impound im•POWND
(to seize and hold in legal custody)
"Nevertheless, the mask has been impounded and will be subject to complete tests as to its functioning ability."

impregnable   im•PREG•nu•bull
(not able to be taken by force)

It was on the crests of the Kyrenia Mountains that the Crusaders built some of their most impregnable fortresses.

imprimatur   im•pruh•MAT•ur
(approval)

"A church funeral is a kind of imprimatur on the Catholic life of a faithful person," said the Rev. Edwin O'Brien, vice chancellor of the archdiocese.

impromptu   im•PROM•too
(without preparation or advance thought; offhand)

"When are we ever going to finish this," the Pope said jokingly toward the end of his impromptu remarks after delivering his written text.

impunity   im•PYU•na•tee
(freedom from punishment)

At the same time, Israeli military forces have been striking at Palestinian targets in southern Lebanon with virtual impunity since Egypt signed the peace treaty with Israel.

impute   im•PYOOT
(to attribute; charge with)

Arabs consider dogs a low form of animal life, and imputing canine characteristics to a person is viewed as particularly insulting.

inadvertent   in•ad•VURT•ent
(unintentional)

Word of the kidnapping inadvertently got out Wednesday morning to some reporters who chanced to monitor a police radio bulletin describing three men wanted for questioning in the abduction, but at the request of the police the story was withheld.

incarcerate
in•KAR•sir•ate
(imprison)

More than 2,100 people are incarcerated in 1,800 cells at Holmesburg, the House of Correction and the Detention Center.

incendiary
in•SEN•dee•er•ee
1. (causing or designed to cause fires)

Five minutes after the flames were reported by an employee at 4:36 P.M., an anonymous male caller warned an Altman's telephone operator of an incendiary device in the building.

2. (emotionally inflaming)

On this occasion, the broadcast will cover both sides of the incendiary issue of abortion.

incessant
in•SESS•ent
(constant)

The doorbell of the Kopelevs' sixth-floor apartment on First Airport Street rings incessantly, their telephone having been disconnected by the secret police years ago.

incisive
in•SIGH•siv
(sharp)

"Discussing government problems with him can be an experience. He may be perceptive and incisive, or he may have a completely blank look as if he never heard of what you are talking about."

incongruous
in•KON•gruh•us
(out of keeping; inconsistent; contrary)

They call her Lady Gottlieb, an incongruous title for a 60-year-old Jewish immigrant from Hungary who speaks English and Hebrew with a Yiddish accent and is the epitome of the Jewish mama.

incorrigible
in•KOR•uh•jeh•bull
(unreformable; uncontrollable)

Mr. Moon, a brilliant drummer and one of rock's most incorrigible clowns, has died since then.

incredulous   in•KREJ•uh•less
(showing disbelief)
Informed that the incumbent, Gov. Cliff Finch, was not a candidate — Mississippi is a one-term state — the farmer looked incredulous. "He ain't running?" he asked.

inculcate   in•KUL•kate
(to teach persistently and earnestly)
It is what makes me like being a teacher, for as a teacher I strive not only to inculcate facts in the minds of my students; more importantly, I try to help them develop values and ethics and a sense of what being human means.

incumbent   in•KUM•bent
(currently in office)
During the Democratic primary in which she upset the incumbent, Arthur Blyn, and again in the general election, Mrs. Lambert ran an aggressive advertising campaign.

incur   in•KUR
(bring upon oneself)
Marino, who was a star football and baseball player in high school, became interested in bicycling as part of a rehabilitation program for a back injury he incurred while lifting weights.

incursion   in•KUR•zhen
(a sudden brief invasion or raid)
A military source said that Israeli villages had been shelled from that region and it had been a point of departure for incursions across the border.

indelible
in•DEL•eh•bull
(permanent; uneraseable)
It doesn't take much for a performer to establish himself indelibly in the public mind, once and for all, now and forever, amen.

indigenous
in•DIJ•uh•nuss
(native)
With the possible exception of the improving Denver Symphony, there is not a single first-class orchestra indigenous to the Rockies, but summertime here has become a music lover's paradise.

indigent
IN•dih•jent
(poor)
The 36-year-old physician offered his services to Los Angeles County officials after Gov. Edmund G. Brown Jr. had proposed that, in return for a state-supported fund to reduce the cost of malpractice insurance, physicians be required to treat the indigent and patients in areas with few or no doctors.

indiscriminate
in•dis•KRIM•eh•net
(not discriminating; chosen at random)
Strings of firecrackers were tossed indiscriminately into crowds, forcing frightened and screaming shoppers to move briskly along the sidewalks.

indomitable
in•DOM•it•eh•bull
(not easily defeated; unyielding)
With the power part of the Boston batting order coming up, it appeared that the Red Sox might score more runs off the tiring Guidry, but the indomitable left-hander induced an inning-ending double-play grounder from Fred Lynn, the American League's leading run producer.

inebriated   in•EE•bree•ate•ed
(drunk)

The big difference between inebriated people and animals, the wildlife organization notes, is that humans often set out deliberately to addle or dull their senses, while animals are taken unawares.

ineffectual   in•uh•FEK•choo•uhl
(unable to produce the desired effect)

"People have said a lot of bad things about Nixon. They called him a liar and a cheat and a crook. But they never called him ineffectual. Ineffectual is just about the worst thing you can say about a President, and it's what people are saying about Carter."

inept   in•EPT
(clumsy or bungling; without skill)

The dead flowers on the tables and the inexcusable background music, plus the indifferent, inept service and only moderately good food made it hard to believe that this is really one of the 19 best restaurants in France.

inertia   in•ER•sha
(inaction)

She said that because of American "bureaucratic inertia," the United States had been receiving only 4,000 to 5,000 refugees a month.

inexorable   in•EK•ser•eh•bull
(unalterable)

Not for the mighty hen such trifling speculation as whether she or the egg comes first. She knows too well the inexorable decree of nature that the egg comes first, being served at breakfast, while the chicken is reserved for dinner.

inextricable   in•EKS•tri keh•bull
(that cannot be disentangled or untied)

The name of Robert Moses is tied inextricably to this place; Mr. Moses, who is now 91 and retired from public life, is the sole reason Jones Beach is as it is.

influx IN•fluks
(a flowing in)
Headline: Woodside Rages Over Influx of Illegal Aliens.

infrastructure IN•fra•struk•chur
(a substructure of underlying foundation; esp. the basic installations and facilities on which the continuation and growth of a community, state, institution, etc. depend)
"While the infrastructure can't cushion every bounce, you are dealing with a fairly well-organized institution in OPEC."

inherent in•HAIR•ent
(inborn)
"If military service is to be considered a duty inherent in citizenship, then why for some and not for all?"

initiate in•ISH•ee•ate
(to begin; set going)
The New York area blackout initiated by lightning two years ago this month is estimated to have cost more than $350 million, and a wider blackout would be a national catastrophe.

injunction in•JUNK•shun
(an order or writ from a court prohibiting a person or group from carrying out an action, or ordering an action to be done)
Judge Robert L. Taylor fined five workers $400 each for being on the picket line yesterday afternoon and this morning in defiance of his injunction prohibiting picketing.

innocuous   i•NAHK•yoo•wus
(inoffensive; harmless)

The House of Representatives calendar for Tuesday included an innocuous-sounding bill that would extend school lunch programs for two years. The only problem was that the tentative Federal budget adopted last month proposed cutbacks in the program worth more than $500 million, and it appeared to some that school lunch backers were trying to slip the bill through before the budget-cutters could start snipping away at the program.

innovation   in•uh•VAY•shun
(something newly introduced)

The most recent innovation on the aircraft carrier is fast foods.

inordinate   in•OR•din•et
(more than should be expected; excessive)

And guests at crowded functions complained of inordinate delays in retrieving their valet-parked automobiles.

insidious   in•SID•ee•us
(more dangerous than seems evident; treacherous)

Asbestos is by admission of the nation's top health official, Joseph A. Califano Jr., "one of the most dangerous and insidious substances in the workplace."

insouciant   in•SOO•see•unt
(calm and unbothered)

With an insouciant wave of their shotguns, they intimate that they wish Marcel to stand aside.

insurgent   in•SER•jent
(a member of a rebel force engaged in armed resistance)

The countryside is almost entirely under the control of insurgents.

intangible   in•TAN•juh•bull
(incapable of being perceived by the sense of touch)
Mr. Exton feels that intangible factors, such as boredom, problems with supervisors or merger rumors, can add to the incidence of clerical errors.

intercession   in•tur•SESH•un
(an interposing or pleading on behalf of a person in difficulty or trouble)
He was released from prison in 1974 through the intercession of Amnesty International and Rumanian officials.

interloper   in•tur•LO•pur
(one who thrusts oneself into the affairs of others)
In the evening, sturdy young men took up positions near the microphone to keep interlopers from grabbing it.

intermediary   in•tur•MEE•dee•eh•ree
(go-between; mediator)
"It's a necessity for them to get their heads together. They don't need me as an intermediary."

interminable   in•TUR•mi•neh•bull
(seemingly endless)
There are 600 horses on the streets of Mackinac, and the smells of lilac and manure mingle in the interminable dusk of northern Michigan.

intermittent   in•ter•MIT•uhnt
(stopping and starting again at intervals; periodic)
When the manager trotted out with the lineup card before the start, everyone stood and began waving at him. A father held up his son above the crowd. Martin waved back, intermittently stopping his discussion with the umpires to tip his cap.

intimidate
(inspire with fear)

in•TIM•uh•date

"I've come this year thinking I have a chance to win," Miss Austin said. "She's not going to intimidate me. I'm ready for her. I'm not saying I'm going to win, I'm just saying I'm not going to let her intimidate me."

intone
(chant; say as though part of a ritual)

in•TONE

He said the aims of the society were clear in the daily prayer intoned by its members: "God make us so strong that nobody should be able to subdue us, but make our character so noble that the world should bow down before us."

intransigent
(uncompromising; inflexible)

in•TRAN•seh•jent

Once again intransigence in Washington has required the formation of special interest groups that should never have been necessary, including one called Agent Orange Victims International.

intrepid
(fearless; dauntless)

in•TREP•id

As Muriel Levitt noticed, inflation has hit more than fuel and food prices. Inevitably, it has also affected clothing costs. But intrepid shoppers are finding ways to do battle.

intrinsic
(inherent)

in•TRIN•zik

In the 30-minute category, Michael Leeson was awarded $10,000 for his "Blind Date" episode of ABC's "Taxi" situation comedy. His script was cited for its "insight into the intrinsic lovability of each human person despite any appearances to the contrary, and for its affirmation of the supreme value of kindness and compassion."

introspection   in•truh•SPECK•shun
(a looking into one's own mind, feelings, etc.; observation and analysis of oneself)

After what aides describe as months of introspection and reading, reinforced by the meetings at Camp David with 150 leaders from various walks of life, Mr. Carter is now saying that the nation is at a crossroads and faces a critical choice.

inundate   IN•un•date
(flood)

At the 1960 Olympics newsmen were inundated for the first time by a daily flood of computerized literature — results, times, scores, schedules.

inure   in•YOOR
(accustom)

Even sadder than the mess is the way New Yorkers appear to have become inured to it.

inveterate   in•VET•er•it
(firmly established by long continuance)

He also enjoys a good cigar, a penchant that could lead to his first conflict with Treasury Secretary-designate Miller, an inveterate nonsmoker.

invulnerable   in•VUL•nur•eh•bull
(immune to attack)

Borg was invulnerable. He retrieved overheads and volleys and hit passing shots on the run as if without effort.

irascible   i•RAS•eh•bull
(easily angered; quick-tempered)

If the irascible McEnroe is developing a reputation for abrasiveness, he also has shown, as he did this afternoon, that he can rise to big occasions.

irony EYE•ruh•nee
(an outcome of events contrary to what was expected)
The irony of having Mr. Baryshnikov perform in Peking, when he defected from the Soviet Union, has not been lost on the Chinese.

irreparable i•REP•ur•eh•bull
(that cannot be repaired)
This insidious disorder, which afflicts some 25 million Americans and often produces no symptoms until it has done irreparable damage, can lead to kidney failure, stroke and heart disease.

irrepressible i•rih•PRESS•eh•bull
(incapable of being repressed or restrained)
He also developed irrepressible business instincts, talents that found full expression in his management of his family's economic empire, said to be worth about $300 million.

irrevocable i•REV•eh•kuh•bull
(unable to be revoked, recalled or undone)
If the party leadership endorsed a Socialist prime minister, the party would be split, perhaps irrevocably.

itinerant eye•TIN•er•ent
(traveling from place to place, esp. for business purposes)
NEW DELHI, July 22 — Beneath an overpass in the heart of this city there is a squatter village of 2,000 itinerant entertainers — jugglers, puppeteers, animal trainers, traditional balladeers and magicians.

itinerary eye•TIN•uh•rer•ee
(a plan for a journey)
The two-year itinerary calls for 95 days in Western Europe, 20 days in the Soviet Union and Eastern Europe, 65 days in the Orient, 15 days in the Middle East and 55 days in the Americas.

jargon   JAR•gun
(the specialized vocabulary of those in the same work, profession, etc.)

In the jargon of the bond community, "The technicals held up the market most of the day."

jaunty   JAWN•tee
(having an easy confidence; perky)

Yesterday, when the jury recommended the death sentence, Mr. Bundy reacted with jauntiness and composure. "See you next trial," he said with a grin, waving to the courtroom crowd.

jovial   JO•vee•ull
(full of good humor; genial)

The terrorists appeared on the upper balcony in an apparently jovial mood.

judicious   joo•DISH•us
(wise and careful; showing good judgment)

While few Americans have simply stopped driving, many are planning their trips more judiciously.

juncture   JUNGK•chur
(a particular moment in the development of events)

The crucial juncture came in the third set when Borg was broken in the ninth game and fell behind by 5-4.

junta   HOON•tuh
(a small group ruling a country, esp. immediately after a coup d'état and before a legally constituted

government has been instituted)
The junta has said it wants to install a democratic government with a non-aligned foreign policy and full guarantees of individual liberties.

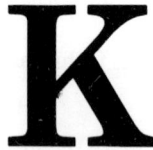

kiosk — KEE•osk
(a small, independently-standing street structure, such as a newsstand, open at one or more sides)
All are on sale in the Victorian-style kiosk at the 60th Street and Fifth Avenue entrance to the park that has been set up as an information and sales center.

labored — LAY•buhrd
(made or done with great effort)
In recent months, Mr. Brezhnev's speech has been labored and slurred.

lackadaisical lak•uh•DAY•zi•kull
(without determination; showing a lack of interest)

The story of his 4-week-long illness is one of early misdiagnosis, apparently because of lackadaisical efforts by two Long Island physicians, followed by a 71-year-old pediatrician's success in solving the mystery.

lackey LAK•ee
(a follower who carries out another's orders like a servant)

The same voice has now scored a hit with a song that goes: "Bakhtiar, Bakhtiar, you irresponsible lackey, you loafer, you source of shame, you donkey, you lover of cucumber peels."

lackluster LAK•lus•tur
(lacking brilliance, radiance, liveliness, etc.; dull)

I've always worn the most fashionable sneaker, except for a brief period during my lackluster college basketball career.

laconic luh•KON•ik
(using few words)

Over breakfast at his hotel he was laconic and unsmiling as he picked at his food.

laid back LAYD•BAK
(relaxed; easygoing)

"The Lone Star has become too fashionable now," Miss Parker contends. "It used to be laid back, but now it's chic. After Willie Nelson took some of the 'Saturday Night Live' crowd there, it started becoming another fancy Village hangout."

lament lah•MENT
(to feel or express sorrow or regret for)

"Right now I'm going on what I see," Torre said, lamenting the fact that he has had fine efforts the last two nights from Hassler and Dock Ellis and no hitting to go with it.

languish   LANG•gwish
(to undergo neglect)
The others also reported having languished in detention centers for periods of up to three years before being convicted, a common problem in China in recent years.

lanky   LAN•kee
(awkwardly tall and lean)
In today's center-court feature, Hank Pfister, a lanky Californian with a hard serve and formidable forehand, was outclassed by Borg.

latent   LAYT•ent
(lying hidden and undeveloped within a person or thing)
The latent danger of a world monetary crisis has been brought close to the surface again.

lateral   LAT•uh•rul
(sideways)
"I had no lateral movement in the arm. I could punch straight up like this —" elbow tight to his side, he threw a short uppercut — "but I couldn't swing a round punch."

latitude   LAT•uh•tood
(freedom from narrow restrictions)
While the Chiefs are responsible to the President, as

their Commander in Chief, they traditionally have had a certain latitude in expressing their own views before Congress.

laud   LAWD
(to praise)
HEADLINE: Rhodesia Lauds U.S. Senate's Vote

leech   LEECH
(a person who clings to another to get what he can from him; parasite)
Outside, perhaps a dozen friends, admirers and leeches were waiting for an audience.

leery   LEAR•ee
(on one's guard; wary; suspicious)
So many people are leery of food additives and of excess fat that the very thought of a sausage is enough to fill them with dread, and the eating of it fills them with guilt.

lethal   LEE•thul
(deadly)
But Pecci, as he had done so often during the tournament, brought out his lethal serve for the crucial points.

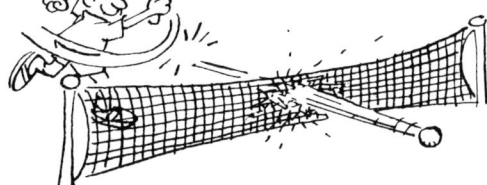

lethargy   LETH•ur•jee
(a great lack of energy)
Stock prices eased again in subdued trading yesterday as investor lethargy hung as heavy on the market as the heat of the day.

leviathan   li•VIE•uh•thun
(a whale)

During World Wars I and II, human beings were so busy slaughtering each other that they had no time to hunt the harmless leviathans who would otherwise have ended up as pet food and cosmetics.

lionize   LIE•eh•nize
(to treat as a celebrity)

Up in her home town of Rockland, Me., yesterday, Louise Nevelson was lionized as Rockland's most famous citizen, and for the first time there, a major exhibit of her work opened, at the Farnsworth Museum.

litany   LIT•en•ee
(a dreary or repetitive recital or account)

An almost constant litany from Camp David has been the reports of the President's excellent health and spirits.

literally   LIT•ur•eh•lee
(actually; in fact)

One sign of the state of his Congressional relations is that the Democratic Senators literally weren't listening. They were at their annual dinner in the Capitol's Caucus Room and no one had brought a television set.

lithe   LIGHTH
(limber; supple)

The tall boyish-looking musician entered the room lithely and sat at the grand piano.

litigation   lit•uh•GAY•shun
(a lawsuit)

Mr. Shattuck, in response to a question, said that the A.C.L.U. was considering "necessary litigation" against the Navy to end its policy.

loathe LOWTHE
(to feel intense dislike for; detest)

Mozart loathed the flute, but that fact did not prevent him from composing several delightful works featuring the instrument.

loathsome LOWTHE•sum
(disgusting)

Anti-Semitism took some of its most loathsome forms in the Latvia of his childhood, and his mother made up her mind that there was only one place for herself and her children: the United States.

logistics loh•JISS•tiks
(calculations)

"General ideas are all very well in politics," she said, "but if they're not translated into specifics and logistics, they solve nothing."

longevity lawn•JEV•ut•ee
(length of life)

"Guys like Brock, McCovey and Yastrzemski have one thing in common: They're in great shape. Your mental outlook is the key to your physical condition, and your body is obviously the key to your longevity."

lucid LOO•sid
(characterized by clear perception and expression)

According to American officials who attended the three days of meetings with President Carter, Mr. Brezhnev is still the man in charge, still lucid in his better moments, still the pre-eminent figure.

lucrative LOO•kruh•tiv
(profitable)

A new eruption of terrorist violence in Spain is threatening tourism, the country's most lucrative industry.

M

magnitude
(size)
MAG•nuh•tood

A sense of the magnitude of the total waste problem can be gained by examining the amount produced by an average reactor in a single year.

magnum opus
(a person's greatest work or undertaking)
MAG•nuhm•OH•puhs

Trained as a philosopher, he plans to work on two books, one on "the 20 greatest instrumental soloists," and "a magnum opus on the quality of greatness in art."

malady
(illness)
MAL•uh•dee

Travelers' diarrhea is a poorly understood malady.

malaise
(mental uneasiness or discomfort)
mal•LAZE

No matter who finally proves able to form it, a new government in New Delhi is unlikely to dispel the malaise that has demoralized the country since it regained its political freedom two years ago.

malcontent   MAL•cun•tent
(a discontented, dissatisfied or rebellious person)
Congress's purpose in life is to get re-elected, which it does by running chores for back-home moneybags and malcontents, and it gets offended if asked to interrupt its self-service to deal with large problems.

malicious   muh•LISH•us
(intentionally harmful; spiteful)
"But the Sandinista guerrilla is a humanist, not a terrorist, as he is often maliciously portrayed in the international press."

mandate   MAN•date
(the wishes of constituents expressed through an election and regarded as an order)
When turnout in a Presidential election falls to barely 50 percent, serious questions must rise about the validity of the mandate.

martyr   MAR•tur
(one who endures great suffering on behalf of any belief, principle or cause)
Mr. Davis, 32 years old, was dubbed the "marijuana martyr" by Rolling Stone magazine after a Wythe County judge in 1974 sentenced him to 20 years in prison for possessing marijuana and another 20 years for intending to distribute it.

mausoleum   maw•suh•LEE•um
(a building with vaults for the entombment of a number of bodies)
No one can be buried in the mausoleum just yet, however. Like any other new building, it needs a certificate of occupancy from the city.

maverick   MAV•uh•rik
(a person who takes an independent stand, refusing to conform to that of his party or group)
The 51-year-old maverick is still angry and is still

maxim   MAK•sum
(an expression of a general truth or principle)
Always be dynamic, especially if you don't plan to do much, goes the old political maxim.

maze   MAZE
(a confusing, intricate network of pathways)
He believes the truckers are faced with a most unfair maze of weight regulations that, he says, cost them money or force them to break the law.

meander   me•AN•dur
(wander aimlessly)
His performances of his own compositions are apt to fall into meandering patterns that run out of steam when they are stretched too far.

mecca   MEK•uh
(any place visited by many people)
The Virginian-Pilot, Norfolk's morning newspaper, said in its lead editorial yesterday that the center would be a "mecca for sightseers as well as environmentalists and oceanographers."

mediocre   mee•dee•OH•kur
(neither good nor bad; ordinary)
The food was mediocre, the service agonizingly slow and the mood disrupted by piped-in music.

megalomania   meg•low•MAY•nee•ah
(an obsession with doing grand things)
"Our Hitler," the final section of a trilogy by Mr. Syberberg on the rise of fascism in Germany, attempts to explore Hitler's megalomania and its relation to German culture and mythology.

megalopolis   meg•uh•LOP•uh•less
(an urban region consisting of several large cities and suburbs that adjoin each other)
On Route 281 north of San Antonio, the megalopolis has not yet come in and cattle and goats continue to graze.

mélange   may•LONZH
(a mixture; medley)
Another friend informs me that in New Zealand, if you serve any kind of fruit mélange and omit the passionfruit, it causes heads to turn in wonder.

melee   MAY•lay
(a confused, general, hand-to-hand fight among a number of people)
The New York Yankees got into another bench-clearing melee and again lost to the Milwaukee Brewers today.

memento   me•MEN•toh
(something that serves as a reminder of what is past or gone)
Lee Mazzilli left the hospital today with lingering amnesia, a headache, a cut cheekbone and a black eye—mementos of his spectacular outfield collision with Dan Norman—and flew home to New York to await the return of the Mets.

memorabilia mem•uh•ruh•BILL•ee•uh
(souvenirs)

Who else could auction off Reggie Bars for 100 bucks a bite and loot the Yankee locker room that afternoon and auction off Billy Martin's shirt, along with other Yankee memorabilia?

mendacious men•DAY•shuss
(not truthful; lying)

Fresh farm produce will once again be available for people who would rather *eat* that vine-ripened tomato or sweet corn-on-the-cob than read about it on some mendacious menu.

menial MEE•ni•uhl
(pertaining to unskilled work)

"They take the menial jobs that no one else is willing to take," he asserted, "and they are a benefit to our economy."

mentor MEN•tor
(a wise and trusted teacher or counselor)

He learned the business from the bottom up, "and he really learned it," recalls his mentor, Robert V. Roosa, now a partner at Brown Brothers, Harriman in New York.

mercurial mur•KYUR•ee•ull
(changeable; fickle; erratic)

The Socialist's opponents argue that Mr. Soares's mercurial behavior contributed importantly to the sagging prestige of party government.

mesmerize MEZ•muh•rize
(to spellbind or fascinate as by hypnosis)

Sun worshippers retired to the Monte Carlo Beach Club, known as Le Beach. Despite such diversions, the antiques dealers kept on the job, mesmerized by the contents of the collection.

metaphor
MET•uh•for
(a figure of speech)

"In terms of reacting to direction, it's as though I went into another gear," he said, which isn't a bad metaphor, since in "Breaking Away" he plays the father of a youth who wants to be a bicycle racer.

métier
MET•tyay
(field of work in which one has special ability; forte)

"We're not out to capture the Academy Awards," Mr. Broccoli replied, "we're out to make an entertainment. For instance, we're not out to prove various things about Vietnam. That isn't our métier, we don't know how to do "The Deer Hunter" and films like that."

metric ton
MEH•trik•tun
(2,204.62 pounds)

In 1978, the world harvested a record 1.19 billion metric tons of grain.

milieu
meel•YOO
(environment)

If you sometimes weary of catching saltwater fish with rod and line, enter their milieu and go hunting for them.

millennium
muh•LEN•ee•um
(a period of 1,000 years)

HEADLINE: Isle of Man Marks Millennium Of Its Parliament With Style.

mime   MIGHM
(a pantomimist)

In Minneapolis, a huge crowd gathers during a festival to watch as a mime feels for an opening along the imaginary wall that surrounds him.

minimalist   MIN•uh•muh•list
(in the arts, the use of the fewest elements to achieve a desired effect)

In addition, his minimalist acting recalls, at its best, the pared-down techniques of such bygone worldwide favorites as Gary Cooper.

minimize   MIN•uh•mize
(to estimate or make appear to be of the least possible amount, value, or importance)

Mr. Mondale, in his statement, minimized the reports and said: "Despite scattered incidents of violence, I am informed by top Justice Department officials that the roads are open and safe."

minuscule   MIN•us•kyool
(tiny)

He did stress that the mines, which are carried on Carbide's books at $25 million, had made a "minuscule" contribution to corporate profits.

minute   my•NOOT
(tiny)

However, over the years minute residues of the drug continued to be found in many cattle and sheep.

misdemeanor   mis•duh•MEE•nur
(a criminal offense defined as less serious than a felony)

A second section of the law declares that "no person shall operate a motor vehicle while he is in an intoxicated condition." That is a misdemeanor, punishable by a jail term of up to a year.

mishap   MIS•hap
(an unfortunate accident)

McEnroe, despite having fractured his nose in a swimming-pool mishap last Saturday, says he is playing as well as ever these days, and he looks it.

misnomer   mis•NO•mur
(a misapplied name)

The term "synthetic" is actually something of a misnomer. The oil is there. It's just hard to take it out of the shale and tar sands or to convert it from coal.

mitigate   MIT•uh•gate
(to make less severe)

"Man is setting in motion a series of events that seem certain to cause a significant warming of the world climate over the next decades unless mitigating steps are taken immediately," the report declared.

mockery   MAHK•eh•ree
(ridicule)

A depiction of a child being vaccinated struck other museumgoers as a mockery of the Nativity.

modus vivendi   mo•dus•vi•VEN•dee
(a manner of living or getting along)

Determined to resolve this unsatisfactory situation, the United States hit upon the ingenious idea of using scientific cooperation as the basis for a modus vivendi.

momentum   mo•MENT•um
(force or speed of movement)

The Mets' momentum stopped yesterday. They won a game.

monolith   MON•eh•lith
(a single massive block or piece of stone)

The shafts beneath the gray concrete monoliths are being sunk at the rate of about six feet a day.

moratorium   mawr•a•TAW•ree•um
(a temporary, authorized stopping of activity)

The International Whaling Commission has called for a worldwide moratorium on whaling by factory ships, which account for most of the slaughter.

mores   MORE•aze
(a society's generally accepted customs and ways which have grown out of its fundamental beliefs)

Some day, historians from outer space will be studying the social mores of a planet named Earth, and they will get to a little community named Southampton and shake their helmets and waggle their antennas in bewilderment.

morose   muh•ROHS
(gloomily ill-tempered)

Many officials, deeply resentful of the foreign press, sit in the bar morosely all afternoon, then try to pick quarrels with reporters. The journalists, who have learned to spot revolvers hidden under shirts, smile diplomatically and turn away.

motif   mo•TEEF
(a repeated figure in a design)

A low thatched roof covers all but the stilt supports of the dwelling and the doorway is accessible only by a ladder that can be withdrawn, keeping out unwanted visitors. Simple motifs are carved into the posts or the beams.

muckrake   MUK•rake
(to search for and expose real or alleged corruption, scandal or the like, esp. in politics, and to publicize it in the press)

Le Canard Enchaine, a satirical weekly that goes in for muckraking, carries a facsimile of the President's tax form, but doesn't say how it came by it.

muse   MYOOZ
(to think or say meditatively)
Mr. Deutsch swats a mosquito and muses over his luck in finding an island with a fully equipped movie studio and no automobiles.

muted   MYOOT•ed
(lowered in intensity; softened)
Although the debate over the readiness of the volunteer Army and its future has intensified in Congress and within the Defense Department, the controversy seems muted at Fort Hood, a 3339-square-mile base that is the Army's largest in the nation, with more than 41,000 soldiers.

myriad   MIR•ee•ud
(countless; innumerable)
There are myriad theories to explain the decline in proms, ranging from alienation to inflation, but at John Bowne about one-quarter of the senior class of 800 did attend.

nadir   NAY•dir
(the lowest point)
These days may not be the nadir of Jimmy Carter's fortunes as President of the United States, but they are certainly the lowest point thus far.

nebulous
NE•byuh•luhs
(vague; indistinct)

The Ramones are so blank and nebulous on screen that they never emerge as individuals, in the manner of the Beatles in *their* films.

nefarious
ni•FAIR•ee•us
(extremely wicked; villainous)

"We are in the mailing-list business," Mr. Ginzburg said. "There's nothing nefarious in that."

neophyte
NEE•uh•fite
(a beginner; novice)

Anyone who has learned to play the piano using Bela Bartok's music for children or other neophytes realizes how distinctive it is.

nepotism
NEP•uh•tizm
(favoritism shown to relatives, esp. in appointment to desirable positions)

Since its beginning 10 years ago, the sewer project has been fraught with cost overruns and charges of corruption, nepotism and mismanagement.

niggardly
NI•gurd•lee
(stingy; miserly)

In Foreign Relations Committee hearings, both liberal and conservative critics attacked the Strategic Arms Limitation Treaty's gifts as niggardly.

noncommittal non•kuh•MIT•el
*(not committing oneself to a particular
point of view or course of action)*

In Arlington, Tex., where the Yankees lost to the Rangers last night, Lemon was noncommittal. "I haven't been notified of anything yet," said the man who led the team to the World Series victory last year. "I'll wait and see what happens."

nondescript non•di•SKRIPT
*(so lacking in recognizable character or qualities
as to belong to no definite class or type)*

At the center of it all here in the dairy country of northern Vermont, where the cows outnumber the people, is a nondescript brick building designed to treat whey, a smelly gray-green liquid byproduct of cheese that used to be the state's major source of water pollution.

novice NAH•vis
(a person new to a particular activity)

Those who ran in last year's marathon, in which there were 9,875 starters and 8,588 finishers, have been asked to stand aside this year so that more novices may enter.

obsolete ob•suh•LEET
(out-of-date)

Believing that token sellers and turnstiles were obsolete, D.C. transit planners chose to install machines that dispense something called farecards in exchange for dollar bills.

obstinate   AHB•stuh•nit
(stubborn)

Despite the 18-month price freeze, the world economy remains obstinately stuck in the inflationary doldrums with unemployment now slightly higher than it was at the time of the 1977 Stockholm meeting.

obstreperous   ub-STREP•uh•rus
(unruly)

One of the sailors, an assistant professor at Yale, became drunk and obstreperous, in that order, and pursued a young woman with such zeal that he had to be restrained.

octogenarian   ahk•tuh•ji•NAIR•ee•uhn
(someone 80 years old, or between the ages of 80 and 90)

And Walter Hoving, the octogenarian chairman of Tiffany & Company, suffered the ultimate humiliation working for an insurance company. He got fired.

odyssey   AH•duh•see
(an extended wandering or journey)

Brown's odyssey this season has taken him from the Mets to the Blue Jays to San Juan to Columbus to the Yankees.

ominous   AH•muh•nus
(like an evil omen; threatening; sinister)

An ominous foretaste of the future came in a report that three United States oil companies have increased profits from Alaskan drilling by 70 percent this year already, because, as is traditional, they have followed OPEC in its hikes.

omnipresent ahm•ni•PRE•zuhnt
(always present)

Interior decorator Gloria Rothfeld, of Great Neck, N.Y., also observes that there is the feeling of being pressured by the omnipresence of the work desk. "I walk into my apartment and see the desk and I have to work to clear it up, which may mean working 14 hours a day," she said.

omniscient ahm•NI•shuhnt
(knowing all things)

"The President is the elected chief executive of our Government, not an omniscient leader cloaked in mystical powers."

onerous OWN•uh•russ
(burdensome)

Shooters thus must choose a rifle that is powerful enough to accomplish this but not so powerful that, because of recoil, shooting it in competition is onerous.

opaque oh•PAKE
(not letting light pass through)

His son, also named Michael, leaned over a glass counter containing shoe laces. The years had made the scratched glass opaque.

opportunist op•ur•TOON•ust
(one who is out for gain, regardless of principles or the interests of other people)

As an opportunist betraying his friends and his principles in quest of survival, Mr. McKellen offers additional evidence that he is the finest stage actor of his generation.

optimum OP•tuh•mum
(the greatest degree or best result)

One invention automatically sets a color camera for optimum performance in a matter of seconds.

opulent AH•pyuh•luhnt
(displaying wealth)

The National has spared no expense — or expanse — in outfitting "Undiscovered Country.' Using the entire breadth of the open stage, Peter Wood's production is opulent, with furniture that might set records at Sotheby's and clothes that seem to come from a manorhouse wardrobe rather than a costume shop.

orientation or•ee•un TAY•shun
(adjustment to a situation)

Mr. Riley and his wife watched videotaped films about cancer and laetrile as part of their orientation to the treatment.

ostensible os•STEN•suh•bull
(outwardly appearing as such)

Although the purpose of today's pontifical high mass, indeed the ostensible purpose of his entire visit, was to celebrate the 900th anniversary of Poland's patron saint, John Paul referred only in passing to St. Stanislaus.

ostracize OS•truh•size
(to banish, exclude)

Looking back on a period of several years in which his

acting services, to put it as charitably as possible, were not in demand in films, George Hamilton said one day recently: "When you're cold, you're not ostracized, or anything like that. The cruel thing is that they invite you to their parties, but not to their pictures."

overextend   oh•vuh•rik•STEND
(to extend beyond reasonable limits or beyond one's capacity to meet obligations or commitments)

But Valley Studio overextended itself financially and is in danger of closing.

overt   oh•VURT
(not concealed or secret; open)

An overt operation could take the form of a violent crash attack by well-armed terrorists intent on seizing a B-52 unit on alert status or the underground control capsules and missile squadrons of an ICBM squadron.

P

paean   PEE•un
(a song of joy, triumph, praise, etc.)

Mr. Wayne starred in his first television special, "Swing Out, Sweet Land," a paean of patriotism, in 1970, and later became well-known for various television appearances.

pall   PAWL
(a dark or gloomy covering)

Late at night there is a pall of smoke over the small dance floor, people are mingling and hunting for attachments, and ever more New York than Carolina voices can be heard chiming in with the Mick Jagger lyrics from the juke box.

pallor   PAL•or
(unnatural paleness)
George Lutz (James Brolin) has begun to look shaggy and pink-eyed, and now he has a terrible gray pallor.

panacea   pan•uh•SEE•uh
(a cure-all)
"But I think we should recognize that SALT II is no panacea."

panache   puh•NASH
(style)
Panache these days is not, of course, what it once was, even on, and around the corner from, Fifth Avenue.

pandemonium   pan•duh•MO•nee•um
(wild disorder, noise or confusion)
The lobbies of downtown hotels were scenes of pandemonium as the many Nicaraguans staying in them came down from their rooms to cheer, cry and clasp one another.

pantheon   PAN•thee•on
(the gods or heroes of a particular group)
Where will Leonid Brezhnev rank in the pantheon of Communist heroes?

paradox
PAR•uh•doks
(a seemingly impossible contradiction)
Aalto buildings pull off a rare paradox: they combine intimacy and monumentality.

paramilitary
PAR•uh•MIL•uh•ter•ee
(concerning forces working with, or in addition to, a regular military organization)
Israel decided today to set up six paramilitary agricultural settlements in occupied Arab territories.

paramount
PAR•uh•maunt
(of chief importance)
The corridors that run through its several large cell blocks are dreary and violent. For inmates and guards, rehabilitation is generally a joke. Mere survival is paramount.

pariah
puh•RIGH•uh
(a person rejected by others; an outcast)
The former Prime Minister, who governed India under emergency provisions for 19 months and was subsequently accused of abuse of her power, is still widely regarded as a political pariah.

parlance
PARR•lunts
(language)
In tax parlance, the basis was "stepped up" to $100,000, its market value, from the $50,000 that Mr. Jones, Sr. had paid.

parlay
pahr•LAY
(exploit successfully)
The White Sox parlayed two walks, a hit batsman and three singles into a 4-0 lead in the second inning.

parley
PAHR•lee
(a conference called to settle a particular matter)
Diplomats close to the talks suggested that the parley

parochial · puh•ROH•ki•uhl
(narrow)

To Congressional leaders, the passage of the conservation amendments indicated that many lawmakers are still dominated by parochial concerns on the energy issue and remain reluctant to adopt any rationing or conservation plan that would require sacrifice from their constituents.

parody · PA•ruh•dee
(to imitate for the purposes of satire)

Miss Newman manages to parody a dozen of the best-known pop singers and their mannerisms with verve and humor.

passé · pa•SAY
(out-of-date; old-fashioned)

In any case, say reliable sources in the fashion industry, the deeply slit skirt is already passé.

pastiche · pas•TEESH
(a mixture of things from various sources; potpourri)

In other words, the documentary is a pastiche of science, science fiction and futurist theories.

paternalistic · puh•turn•el•IS•tik
(fatherly)

Nykoluk is low-keyed, soft-spoken and almost paternalistic toward the players while Shero is a more distant figure, although one always on top of the situation.

patronizing   PAY•truh•nighz•ing
(condescending)

Mrs. King is delighted that there are so many Tracy Austins in professional tennis these days. She refers to them as "babycakes," and not patronizingly.

paucity   PAW• si•tee
(scarcity)

A spokesman for Lincoln Center reported that none of the houses there were feeling any pinch attributable to paucity of petrol.

pedestrian   puh•DESS•tree•un
(ordinary and dull)

Dim sum and fried appetizers were pedestrian and the broth for the wonton soup was stingingly salty.

penchant   PEN•chunt
(inclination)

Mr. Fiedler's activity, success and natural penchant for showmanship and publicity did not endear him to most of the other conductors of the Boston Symphony.

pendulous   PEN•juh•lus
(hanging or bending downward; drooping)

Ferns with long pendulous leaves are especially appealing when grown in hanging baskets.

penultimate   pih•NUL•tu•mut
(next to the last)

The penultimate unit in the parade will sail under tow: a floating derrick, a floating hospital and similar craft that need tugs to move.

perceptive pur•SEP•tiv
(having keen insight or intuition; penetrating)
(9) MOVIE: "Three into Two Won't Go" (1969). Rod Steiger, Claire Bloom, Judy Geeson. A marriage dissolves. Coolly perceptive. And British. (2 hrs.)

peregrinations PER•uh•greh•NAY•shuns
(travels from one place to another)
A detailed account of Mr. Wang's peregrinations was published in the Canton newspaper Nanfang.

perennial puh•REN•ee•ull
(returning again and again; yearly)
We learned that while many had cruised before and some were perennial voyagers on the Flavia, many others were novices.

perfunctory pur•FUNG•tuh•ree
(superficial)
The only fight in the clubhouse that made news was a perfunctory scuffle between Cliff Johnson and Rich Gossage.

perimeter puh•RI•muh•ter
(the outer boundary)
Strings of lights go on along the perimeters of settlements, and from a high distance they look like bracelets scattered across waves of black velvet.

peripatetic PER•uh•puh•tet•ik
(moving from place to place)
There have been few gasoline lines in Nebraska so far, and both the farmers and townspeople are as peripatetic as usual.

periphery puh•RIF•uh•ree
(outskirts)
The business, born here on the periphery of Providence, R.I., the country's jewelry capital, has been extremely successful.

perpetual
pur•PECH•uh•wul

(constant; everlasting)

As Commissioner, Mr. Coughlin would supervise more than 21,000 prisoners held in a system of 34 prisons that is perpetually plagued with overcrowding.

perquisite
PER•qwuh•zit

(a privilege or benefit to which a person is entitled by virtue of status or position)

There is no evidence that the party is having trouble recruiting new members. It is still the main path to success in China, offering many perquisites otherwise unavailable: better housing, vacation retreats, chauffeur-driven cars, frequent travel, access to special food stores.

persona
pur•SO•nuh

(the outer personality or facade presented to others by an individual)

Mr. Eastwood's poker-faced acting had long been described as consisting of "four grimaces and two glances"; with the continuing popularity of the Dirty Harry persona, some critics have attacked the actor's politics, as well.

perspective
pur•SPEK•tiv

(point of view)

Since they represented four different perspectives, they were having trouble agreeing on much more than that there was a problem, something that the audience of 40 persons knew well enough.

pervasive
pur•VAY•siv

(spread throughout)

Few people realize just how pervasive an ingredient salt has become in the modern American diet.

phalanx
FAY•langks

(a compact or closely massed body of people or things)

The company's office on 36th Street resembles the chaotic campaign headquarters of a politician, with unmatched, shabby furniture, a phalanx of incessantly ringing phones and a clutter of coffee cups, ashtrays and loose paper.

pied-a-terre
pee•ed•uh•TARE

(a dwelling used only part time)

"Since he only wanted a pied-a-terre to spend a few nights a month in, he bought this place for $10,000 and asked me to do what I could with it," said Mr. Hurst, still amused by the Lilliputian assignment that took a half-year's effort.

pillory
PIL•uh•ree

(to expose to public scorn)

They have made many mistakes and paid for a number of them, yet they have been pilloried as well for things they haven't done.

pious
PIE•us

(seemingly virtuous; originally, sincerely religious)

While politicians piously demand that the betting public be protected from fixers such as Anthony (Big Tony) Ciulla, they condone the systematic financial mugging of fans whose recreational preference happens to be a day at the races instead of a day at the golf links, the yacht club or the tennis court.

pique
PEEK

(to arouse resentment in)

Mr. Nederlander was piqued when he was not renominated to the league's board of governors.

pitfall
PIT•fall

(an unsuspected danger that one may fall into)

She is a potentially valuable pop singer, if she can continue to grow and avoid the many pitfalls of the world of popular music.

pivotal PIV•ut•el
(on which something depends; crucial)

They also agreed that the continued security of the Republic of Korea is pivotal to the preservation of peace and stability in the northeast Asia region.

placard PLAK•ard
(poster)

The students carried placards reading "Go Home Yankees" and "U.S. Stop Unwarranted Interference in Our Affairs."

placate PLAY•kate
(to stop from being angry; appease)

Once within her, the devil can never be driven out, only placated in a ritual that will dissuade him from causing harm.

placebo pla•SEE•bo
(a substance having no pharmacological effect but given merely to satisfy a patient who supposes it to be a medicine)

The nurse's call button apparently is a mere placebo at night, for no one appears when the father presses it.

placid PLASS•ud
(calm)

Miss Austin, who is usually placid, became upset by a line call. "I guess he was sleeping," she said of the linesman.

plaintive PLAYN•tiv
(mournful)

Cradling her guitar, Miss Ziavras sang a variety of Greek numbers, plaintive to rhythmic, then rounded out the set with a group of English folk ballads.

platitude   PLAT•uh•tood
(a commonplace or trite remark)

When children make progress, they want more than such platitudes as, "You're doing great. Keep trying." Once again, the response must be concrete. How many new words have we learned today? What do we know now that we didn't know yesterday?

plebiscite   PLEB•uh•site
(an expression of the people's will by direct ballot on a political issue)

Gov. Carlos Romero Barcelo of Puerto Rico has reported that a poll indicates a plebescite planned for 1981 will produce a strong vote for statehood.

plethora   PLETH•uh•ruh
(overabundance; excess)

Some observers who have followed the gambling craze on the East Coast are wondering whether a plethora of gambling hotels might not be in the offing with an inevitable collapse sometime later.

plight   PLITE
(a sad situation; predicament)

The plight of the "boat people," most of them ethnic Chinese forced to leave Vietnam, seems to be arousing growing concern in this country.

ploy   PLOY
(trick)

According to the department, weekend inspections found 14 other stations selling gasoline to preferred customers only, using such ploys as showing a red flag to indicate they were out of gas but selling to special customers anyway.

plummet   PLUM•ut
(plunge)

While automobile sales in the United States have

plummeted in the wake of gasoline shortages and price increases, West Germany's automobile makers continue to enjoy their best domestic year on record.

pluralism PLOOR•uh•liz•um
(the existence within a society of groups distinctive in ethnic origin, cultural patterns, religion, or the like)

But at the same time, Mr. Carter noted differences separating Moscow and Washington, saying that the United States sought "greater pluralism in and among societies" and "social justice and human rights around the globe."

poignant POI•nyunt
(emotionally touching)

Is it a poignant dance-drama or just a soap opera? Balletgoers tend to label John Cranko's "Eugene Onegin" as either one or the other.

polarize PO•luh•rize
(to separate into diametrically opposed, often antagonistic, viewpoints)

Political opinion is polarized, and many Nicaraguans blame Washington for the destruction of the centrist option.

polyglot POL•i•glot
(a mixture of languages)

While Atlanta has not yet taken on the polyglot, cosmopolitan texture of a New York or San Francisco, neither is it any longer simply the commercial hub of a region historically the most xenophobic in the nation.

ponder PON•dur
(think deeply about)

But in private, many Paraguayans are pondering indications that the 66-year-old Paraguayan strongman is losing his grip after a quarter-century of unchallenged rule.

ponderous   PON•duh•russ
(massive; bulky)

Indeed, smaller cars that looked strange two years ago now seem normal to many people, and the leviathans that looked good then now appear ponderous and bloated to them.

pontificate   pon•TIF•ih•kate
(to speak in a pompous way)

The discussers were writers, performers and directors with impeccable credentials, who were serious enough, but not sufficiently pontifical to restrain themselves from being funny at times.

populism   POP•yuh•liz•um
(the political philosophy of appealing to the ranks of ordinary citizens)

So far, Mr. Carter's solution appears to be any format that permits him to convey his political populism directly to the people. At the "town meetings," for example, he projects a sincerity, informality and quiet humor that usually captivates the audience.

portend   por•TEND
(to foreshadow; indicate)

His doctoral thesis, "Lincoln and the Radicals," was well received in academic circles and was regarded by many as portending a promising career.

portent   POR•tent
(omen)

The start of summer this year has been warm and fine, but strange signs and portents are all about.

posthumous   POS•chuh•mus
(published or presented after the creator's death)

"Lucrezia" was Respighi's last opera, completed in 1935 and produced posthumously in 1963.

posturing   POS•cher•ing
(assuming an attitude merely for effect; posing)

"I think we're going through a necessary, early period of time when there's a lot of sparring, a certain amount of posturing and a certain amount of staking out extreme positions."

potboiler   POT•boy•lur
(a mediocre piece of writing produced merely for money)

But "The Other Side of Midnight," based on another Sheldon potboiler, is high on my list of rib-tickling rotten movies, right between "Hanover Street" and "The Betsy."

potpourri   po•poo•REE
(mixture)

At tonight's opening, which has a $5 cover, entertainment begins at 9 P.M. with a potpourri of comedy and song preceding Miss Sage and featuring Tim Cahill, Lois Melodie, Maggie Anderson and others.

pragmatic   prag•MAT•ik
(practical)

But there are other pragmatic reasons for determining exact details of the point where Skylab re-entered the earth's atmosphere and the debris landing area, also called the footprint.

precarious   pri•KAR•ee •us
(uncertain; insecure)

Customers of a defunct securities firm cannot recover losses by suing the firm's outside auditors for failing to alert Federal regulators to the firm's precarious condition.

precious   PRESH•us
(affectedly delicate or overrefined)

"Part of the difficulty with Mozart, without getting

precious about it, is the tremendous importance of every note — at least in the great works, and K.467 is certainly one of them.

precipitate
pri•SI•puh•tayt
(bring on)

A film short from 1950 in which a husband precipitates his divorce through his addiction to toy trains is a reminder of the electric train craze that once gripped the country.

precocious
pri•KO•shuss
(matured beyond what is normal for the age)

The precocious Brooke Shields will star with 18-year-old Christopher Atkins, hitherto unknown to movie audiences.

pre-empt
pree•EMT
(to take action before anyone else can)

The book deals with a Russian attempt to assure the success of a pre-emptive strike against the United States.

preoccupy
pri•AHK•yoo•pigh
(to absorb or engross to the exclusion of other things)

In the last month, Mr. Brown has been preoccupied with California matters and has made no significant national splash.

prerogative
pri•RAH•guh•tiv
(a prior right or privilege)

Not only can the Senate reject a treaty outright, but it may insist that the treaty be modified. This constitutional prerogative was first asserted in 1795, when the Senate made ratification of John Jay's treaty with Britain contingent on deletion of an article limiting trade with the British West Indies.

pretentious — pri•TEN•chuss
(affectedly grand or superior; ostentatious; phony)
La Tour d'Argent might be recommended for its exceptional duck specialties were it not for its filthy dining room and the pretentious, overbearing staff.

pretext — PREE•tekst
(excuse)
"Of course the Israelis will use it as an additional pretext not to talk to Palestinians," said an aide to President Sadat.

prevail — pri•VAIL
(to be victorious; triumph)
When Borg finally prevailed in the fifth set, winning the tennis title for the fourth straight year, the manager of the Mets was impressed.

prevailing — pri•VALE•ing
(predominant)
The prevailing theory is that the loss of the left pylon caused fatal damage to the hydraulic system that operates the plane's controls.

pristine — pris•TEEN
(unspoiled; untouched; pure)
Someday, when there is an airport and a hotel or two, vacationers will pay a lot of money to escape from their hectic lives for a while to the pristine isolation of Indonesia's Anambas Islands.

privy — PRIV•ee
(privately informed about)
Of course, members of the Soviet elite, which is privy to such information, follow the Senate hearings avidly.

proclivity
(tendency)   proh•KLI•vuh•tee

Over the years, Watson watchers have seen a proclivity for losing the lead in the final stages of a tournament, sometimes on the last nine holes.

procrastinate
(to put off to a future time)   pruh•KRASS•tuh•nate

He is, he conceded, "procrastinating, dreading the moment when I have to audition for all those vice presidents."

proficient
(highly competent)   pruh•FISH•unt

There is a sharp decline in the immaculately proficient service that used to distinguish the great restaurants of Europe.

profiteer
(a person who makes excessive profits, esp. by taking advantage of a shortage of supply to charge exorbitant prices)   prof•uh•TEER

For these and other reasons, Big Oil is embroiled in a crisis of public and political confidence. They are the people you love to hate. Oilmen are perceived as liars, cheats, profiteers and worse.

profligate
(extremely wasteful; recklessly extravagant)   PRAH•fluh•git

The idea of Senator Edward M. Kennedy as a Presidential candidate incensed him because he thought the Massachusetts Democrat was a profligate spender "out of step with the times."

profusion
(a rich supply; abundance)   pruh•FYOO•zhun

All during the 30's, a profusion of light verse and essays poured from her pen and appeared in a diversity of magazines, including The New Yorker.

prohibitive
proh•HI•buh•tiv
(such as to prevent purchase, use, etc.)
Coal can be converted into oil and natural gas, but the costs are still considered prohibitive and the conversion process itself is fraught with environmental problems.

proletarian
pro•luh•TER•ee•un
(a member of the working class)
The first Soviet Spartakiad was organized in 1923 as a proletarian answer to "bourgeois" sports contests, but times have changed even if the name has not.

proliferate
pruh•LIF•uh•rate
(to multiply rapidly)
Mosquitoes the size of wombats proliferated in the stagnant water, and, at night, bullfrog called to bullfrog with the urgency of sex-crazed moose, their numbers multiplying as the days progressed.

prolific
pruh•LIF•ik
(producing in large quantities)
As prolific as ever, the artist continues to churn out work from her Spring Street studio in New York, and has done a number of monumental pieces around the city in the last year alone; the Louise Nevelson Plaza in lower Manhattan was recently named after her.

promontory
PROM•un•toe•ree
(a peak of high land that juts out into a body of water)
As we drove along the waterside, our eyes were drawn again and again to the old fortress walls encircling a rocky promontory that jutted into the sea.

propagate
PROP•uh•gate
(to spread from person to person or from place to place)
The following are among the more blatant untruths being propagated in support of higher energy taxes and tighter controls over voluntary market choices:

propitious   pruh•PISH•us
(indicating a favorable future; auspicious)
Joseph's debut, however, wasn't entirely propitious. He arrived, he claims, with a mere $25. With no place to live and no food, he slept in the Coney Island subway station and petitioned apparel merchants on Delancey Street for work.

proponent   pruh•PO•nunt
(an advocate)
Proponents of nuclear power such as Dr. Alvin Weinberg of the Oak Ridge National Laboratory in Tennessee view it as "that miraculous and quite unexpected source of energy," while opponents such as Anthony Z. Roisman of the Natural Resources Defense Council see it as a "Nuclear monster."

prosaic   pro•ZAY•ik
(dull and ordinary)
Zubin Mehta's account of the same symphony with the New York Philharmonic is considerably less impressive. It's only in the final movement that his penchant for overheated excitement gets a chance to make an effect; earlier on, this is a prosaic, unimaginative performance.

proscribe   pro•SKRIBE
(to forbid the use or practice of)
His last work, "Christophorus," proscribed by the Nazis before it reached the stage, has just received its world premiere in Freiburg.

proselytize   PROS•uh•luh•tize
(to try to convert)
The Bahais have also infuriated the Islamic clergy because they are one of the few religious groups that attempt to proselytize among the Moslems.

prospective   pruh•SPEK•tiv
(potential)

In real life, the man being sentenced was William J. Cody, convicted of gaining entrance to the Pound Ridge home of Mr. Cronyn and Miss Tandy last July by pretending he was a prospective buyer.

prostrate   PRAH•strayt
(flat, with the face downwards)

"Whatever you do, come out fighting," Mr. Hooks was quoted as saying. "The country needs a measure of confidence from you. You have to tell the public we don't lie prostrate in front of OPEC."

protagonist   pro•TAG•uh•nust
(main character)

The protagonist of Mrs. Cheney's novel is a reporter who stumbles onto information that forces him to deal with the question of privacy versus the public's need to know.

protean   PRO•tee•un
(readily assuming different forms)

Of course it is easy to find deficiencies in any musician. Noboby is protean enough to encompass all styles.

protocol   PRO•teh•kol
(the rules of etiquette among diplomats and heads of state)

It was "Anwar" and "Menachem" at the Egyptian-Israeli talks in Alexandria this week, but not without some hesitation on the part of the protocol-conscious Israeli leader.

prototype   PRO•teh•tipe
(model)

In some ways, Arizona sociologists have pointed out, Sun City is a prototype of the kind of community that more and more people will live in as more Americans live longer lives.

provincial   pruh•VIN•chul
(narrowness of outlook; exclusive concern with local matters)

"Provincialism exists all over the country, and the financial community is no exception," he said.

provisional   pruh•VI•shuh•nuhl
(temporary, pending permanent establishment)

Nicaragua's rebel-backed provisional junta formed an 18-member cabinet today made up mainly of businessmen and technocrats.

proviso   pruh•VI•zo
(a condition or stipulation)

Mr. Kennedy agreed to be interviewed with the proviso that he and his staff would have an opportunity to review the questions in advance and that no electronic recording would be made of his remarks.

provocative   pruh•VOK•uh•tiv
(thought-provoking)

"Class Enemy" by Nigel Williams is a serious and provocative play, blessed with fine performances and generally expert staging by Tony Tanner.

proximity   prahk•SI•muh•tee
(nearness)

Despite Canada's proximity to the United States and the absence of a language barrier, Canadian production companies have had scant success over the years in marketing their programs in the United States.

prudent   PROO•dent
(showing good judgment; cautious)

A prudent man, Mr. Holifield has the truck equipped with a radar-detecting device that alerts him to a police radar device ahead on the road.

prurient   PROOR•ee•unt
(characterized by lustful thoughts or desires; lewd)

Positioning herself on a corner, tour guide style, Miss Brownmiller gestured up and down 42d Street, commenting on the prurient points of interest.

pseudonym   SOOD•en•im
(pen name)
During the 1960's, she wrote romance and suspense novels under the pseudonym of Anne Eliot.

pugnacious   pug•NAY•shus
(eager and ready to fight; combative)
Rabbi Moshe Levinger, the leader of a pugnacious group of Orthodox settlers, does not understand how anyone could propose self-government for Arabs in the areas that Israel conquered in 1967.

pulchritude   PUHL•kruh•tood
(physical beauty)
Without a doubt, her most memorable contribution to Muppetdom was the construction of what eventually became the goddess of porcine pulchritude, Miss Piggy.

punctuate   PUNK•chuh•wate
(interrupt)
The morning was punctuated with telephone calls praising him for having reached both milestones with his teeth, appetite and biting wit intact.

pungent   PUN•jent
(sharp to the taste or smell)
Pure white pepper is not as pungent or as aromatic as black pepper.

purge   PURJ
(to rid a nation, political party, etc., of individuals held to be disloyal or undesirable)
Iraq's new President, Saddam Hussein, has begun a major purge, accusing some officials of conspiring

against the Government with the support of outsiders. Arab press reports said today that between 56 and 250 Iraqis had been arrested and that a number of those had already been executed.

purist   PYOOR•ist
(one who practices or demands strict observance of rules, as in language or art)
When she had finally conquered the public's indifference to Bach, she found that she had to contend with purists who insist that Bach should not be played on the piano, and literalists who insist that performers should never stray from the printed note.

purported   pur•POR•ted
(as far as the truth has been able to be ascertained)
Mr. Galante was one of the first bosses of organized crime to purportedly get deeply involved in narcotics trafficking.

pyrotechnics   pigh•ruh•TEK•niks
(in a dazzling fashion, like fireworks)
Marvelous Marvin, as Hagler is called on his Massachusetts boxing license, earned a new nickname, Oo-la-la. That was the basic crowd reaction to his pyrotechnical combination in stopping Roberto Cabrera, a hard-chinned Argentine, at 1 minute 15 seconds of the eighth round.

quaff   KWAHF
(to drink deeply in a hearty or thirsty way)
The 131st rowing of the Henley Royal Regatta con-

cluded today in weather that was as sparkling as the champagne that was quaffed by the winners in the Steward's Enclosure.

quagmire   KWAG•mire
(a difficult or inextricable condition; bog)
Yesterday the traffic-enforcement agents gave out the warnings along the East Side at various intersections on 59th Street, and at such other well-known traffic quagmires as Third Avenue and 57th Street and First Avenue and 60th Street.

qualm   KWAHM
(a feeling of uneasiness as having possibly done something wrong; misgiving)
But today, the President was insisting that he had no qualms or apologies about what he had done or to whom he had done it.

quantum leap   KWAHN•tum LEAP
(a giant step forward)
Color photography has made quantum leaps forward since those first crude attempts.

quarry   KWAWR•ee
(prey)
The spearfisherman's most rewarding quarry along the East Coast is probably the tautog, or blackfish, a chunky, tasty fellow that lives around rocks and does not readily spook when you approach.

quasi   KWAY•sigh
(in a sense or manner; seemingly; as if)
All three projects are arising on land made available by the Public Development Corporation, a quasi-public corporation that manages city-owned land.

quell   KWEL
(put an end to)

The protest was quelled early today when a prison tactical squad herded them into the prison yard.

queue KYOO
(a line of persons waiting to be served)
The Ground, as they call this 11-acre mecca of lawn tennis, was overwhelmed by an attendance of 36,848, stuffed into every nook and cranny. The waiting queue was more than a mile long when the gates opened at noon.

quid pro quo KWID PRO KWO
(one thing in return for another)
With many of the institutions lending to the Picasso show, the Museum of Modern Art will respond on a quid pro quo basis. To the Beaubourg in Paris, from which it is borrowing 16 major Picassos, for example, the Modern Museum will send a loan show of Futurist works, rarely seen in Paris.

quintessential kwint•uh•SEN•shul
(the most perfect embodiment of something)
The Miró Museum, designed by José Luis Sert, is a quintessentially Mediterranean structure — white walls, red tile floors, and soft natural light filling its simple interior spaces.

quip KWIP
(a witty remark)
The Pope's voice faltered and he lacked his normal exuberance, though he delivered a number of characteristic quips.

R

rail   RALE
(to complain violently)
"Danny kept railing at me. 'You're a writer,' he said. 'You should be writing.'"

ramification   ram-uh-fuh•KAY•shun
(a result or consequence branching out from an act)
Financial analysts and some Carter Administration officials are concerned about the political ramifications of the oil prices.

rancor   RAN•kur
(a continuing and bitter hate or ill will)
Presumably contributing to the rancor is the fact that all eight are members of a different tribal group from the Prime Minister.

rapport   ra•PORE
(a close, harmonious or sympathetic relationship)
So strong was his rapport with the people of his state that despite the Democratic Party's enduring strength in the state, they three times elected him Governor — in 1938, 1940 and 1942 — four times elected him Senator, in 1944, 1948, 1954 and 1960.

rarefied   RARE•uh•fighd
(refined, subtle or lofty)
"I guess it's easier to make a big hit in this country with a Romantic concerto — you know, that's the money concerto. But Mozart is much more rarefied, and much more meaningful for me."

rationale rash•uh•NAL
(a statement of reasons)

"As a result, they are able to come up with splendid rationales for why $20-a-barrel-oil is good for us."

raucous RAW•kus
(loud and rowdy)

In a raucous meeting that was interrupted repeatedly by shouts and catcalls from the audience, the New York City Rent Guidelines Board yesterday voted not to pass along fuel costs to tenants in about 150,000 rent-stabilized apartments.

rebuke ri•BYOOK
(to scold sharply; reprimand)

Vice President Mondale rebuked Congress today for beginning its monthlong August recess without making "adequate progress" on President Carter's proposed energy legislation.

recalcitrant ri•KAL•suh•trunt
(stubbornly defiant; hard to handle)

It is a recalcitrant world, but some people seem destined to rule it all the same.

recant ri•KANT
(to formally or publicly renounce one's beliefs or former statements)

Miss Zhang, who was 45 years old when she died, had been arrested in 1975 for criticizing China's radicals, the Gang of Four, and had refused to recant despite being tortured.

recapitulation ree•kuh•pich•uh•LAY•shun
(a summary or brief restatement)

"You should never serve caviar before Hungarian goulash," said Michael Mortimer, chairman of the World Boxing Association championship committee, in a recapitulation of last night's two middleweight fights here.

recede   ri•SEED
(move back)

Receding waters allowed some residents to return to their homes on the Texas coast today, but flooded streets kept thousands more stranded.

recluse   REK•loose
(one who lives a secluded, solitary life)

Miss Pickford, like Greta Garbo, retired at the height of her fame and in later years became virtually a recluse at Pickfair, the mansion Douglas Fairbanks bought her as a wedding present.

rectify   REK•ti•fie
(to set right; correct)

What proposals does Bishop Muzorewa have for rectifying the enormous historic disparity between black and white in land, education, wages, employment, housing and health?

recur   ri•KUR
(to occur again, esp. after some lapse of time)

He has been spending much of the past week, however, flat on his back in pain, suffering from the recurring effects of an old spinal injury.

red herring   red HEH•ring
(something used to draw attention away from the real issue)

"I've never heard of such a request," said Mr. Delizonna. "It's another red herring to try to divert us. We have evidence to support everything I said yesterday."

redolent   RED•el•unt
(smelling)

Somewhat in those years, something occurred that led to personal tragedy for Mrs. Stender and an atmosphere still redolent of fear and uncertainty for her colleagues and family.

redress   ree•DRESS
(satisfaction or compensation for a wrong done)

There was no dispute that the woman had been fired because of her sex. The question was whether the Constitution gave her the right to seek redress.

refurbish   ree•FUR•bish
(to brighten; polish up)

Major projects elsewhere are in Georgia and Colorado, where officials are drawing up plans to refurbish their Statehouses with gold-leaf domes.

reiterate   ree•IT•uh•rate
(repeat)

Senator Howard H. Baker, the Senate Republican leader, today reiterated his objections to what he has called the "fatally flawed" strategic arms treaty signed with the Soviet Union, and he set forth some ideas for changes.

relegate   REL•uh•gate
(assign to an inferior position)

Alice Peurala has been fighting with her supervisors at the United States Steel Corporation's Sputh Works plant here since she became convinced that women employees were being relegated to dead-end jobs.

renaissance   ren•uh•SONTS
(rebirth; revival)

The legitimate theatre along Broadway is also booming. "We're having a renaissance," says Irving W. Cheskin, executive director of the League of Theatre Owners and Producers, an organization representing 39 theatres in the area.

rendezvous   RON•di•voo
(a prearranged, mutually-agreed-upon meeting)

That meeting of Nixon and the Shah—two fallen non-angels—must have been a drama-laden rendezvous.

renounce   ri•NOWNTS
(to give up)

The recent executions in Ghana have brought international protests, apparently forcing the new military Government to renounce further use of capital punishment in its drive to end corruption.

repast   ri•PAST
(a meal)

A boiled ham and endive ravigote salad makes an excellent warm weather dish and can be served as a light repast—lunch, for example—with hot French bread.

repertoire   RE•per•twahr
(the entire range of things in a particular field or art)

New shops selling nothing but freshly baked chocolate chip cookies, pecan-chocolate chip cookies, peanut-butter-chocolate chip cookies, and the rest of the cookie repertoire are rapidly opening up in small space retail locations.

replete   ri•PLEET
(plentifully supplied)

Recent history, officials acknowledge, is replete with examples of dictatorial anti-Communist regimes being replaced eventually by governments that violate human rights as badly.

reprehensible   re•pri•HEN•suh•bull
(deserving of strong blame)

A mayoral veto would be "petty and reprehensible," Borough President Andrew J. Stein of Manhattan said after the unanimous approval by the Board of Estimate.

reputed   ri•PYOOT•ed
(generally supposed)

As a skin wash, the juice of sorrel leaves steeped in water are reputed to make the skin smooth and clear.

rescind — ri•SIND
(to revoke, repeal or cancel an act or law)
"I will not remain in the union for one day," he went on, "unless the decision to expel Popov and Yerofeyev is rescinded."

resolute — REZ•uh•loot
(determined; unwavering)
Appearing pained but resolute at the start of his exile, the deposed Nicaraguan President, Anastasio Somoza Debayle, stood in the sundrenched breezeway of his $500,000 island villa here and declared that it was a Communist conspiracy that cast him from power, not the Nicaraguan people.

restive — RES•tiv
(uneasy; impatient)
Mr. Solomon said the Mayor had been growing increasingly restive and had been especially worried about violence on gas lines.

reticent — RE•ti•sunt
(not inclined to speak freely; reserved)
Mr. Webber is reticent about the value of this salvaged treasure. "In the millions," he said last week, "and I'm not going to say any more than that."

retrospect — RE•truh•spekt
(a looking back on the past)
The 1890's rank, in retrospect, among the golden ages of European literature. With Ibsen, Chekhov, Shaw and Wilde in full production, the drama was in as good shape as it had been for many years.

retrospective — re•truh•SPEK•tiv
(a representative exhibition of the lifetime work of an artist)
A six-film retrospective of the work of Jacques Demy will be presented as part of the Film at the Public series at the Public Theatre starting Tuesday.

reverberate ri•VER•buh•rate
(to re-echo or resound)

For the third time since February, the sound of mortars and machine guns reverberated through the dusty streets of this capital in June as one guerrilla faction attacked another.

rhetoric RET•uh•rik
(while "rhetoric" has in the past referred to the art of speaking and writing effectively, in recent years it has been used more often, esp. in politics, to mean language intended to arouse emotions rather than to appeal to rational thinking)

Mr. Byrd said today that he had discussed "the need on both sides for avoidance of inflammatory rhetoric which can only be counterproductive."

ribald RI•buld
(vulgar or indecent in language)

The conclusion is so unexpected that when the gypsy reveals she is pregnant, some dance-goers have burst into laughter. For them, her revelation is akin to the punch line of a ribald joke.

rife RIFE
(abounding; teeming)

Now the industry is rife with rumors that the company is about to introduce another line of high-powered machines, the Series H, that would compete directly with Amdahl's.

rifle RIE•ful
(to ransack and rob)

A security company guard who celebrated his birthday by rifling his employer's safe probably got away with a much smaller haul than police first believed, the police chief of Marseilles said today.

robust
(strong and healthy) — roe•BUST

Under the Sherman Antitrust Act of 1890, Judge Kaufman observed, there is "a firm national policy that the norm for commercial activity must be robust competition."

roil
(to stir up; make angry) — ROYL

HEADLINE: Australian Mining Town Roiled By Move to Take Skylab Chunk

rout
(to cause to flee) — ROUT

"We showed them that we are through being meek in the face of racist attacks," said one of the Asians who routed the white gang that night. "And they haven't been back here to bother us since."

rudimentary
(elementary) — roo•deh•MEN•ter•ee

Pan American World Airways had to interview 16,000 Americans to fill 400 job openings for flight attendants with at least rudimentary foreign language skills.

sacred cow
(a person or thing regarded as above criticism or attack) — SAY•kred KOW

With his well-known irreverence for sacred cows, Mr. Tugwell was perhaps a perfect choice for the task of supervising the drafting of a model new Constitution.

sacrosanct SAK•ro•sangt
(very sacred, holy or inviolable)
The collective is still a sacrosanct idea of Soviet Communism, one that springs out of the Russian culture and finds reinforcement in modern ideology. The notion that a person should work hard not for his own gain but for the good of the society is a strong ideal here, and perhaps as unattainable as any ideal anywhere.

salty SAWL•tee
(sharp; witty)
When he left San Juan in 1946, Mr. Tugwell was 55, but he remained vigorous, salty and handsome, and refused to take a vacation.

salutary SAL•yuh•ter•ee
(healthy; beneficial)
American withdrawal from South Korea, some Pentagon planners believe, will have a salutary effect on Japan, bringing more money and resources to the military.

sanction SANGK•shun
1. (to authorize or approve)
"These mass violations have got to stop," said Judge Greenberg after finding that officials of the union had sanctioned the walkout despite his ruling Tuesday night that the strike was unlawful.

2. (a coercive measure, usually taken by several nations together, for forcing a nation considered to have violated international law to end the violation)
President Carter said three weeks ago that he would not lift sanctions against the African nation because he did not regard the recent elections installing a biracial government there as free and fair.

sanguine SANG•gwun
(cheerful; optimistic)
Not everyone is so sanguine about the prospects.

sap   SAP
(to weaken)

The officials portray North Korea as a nation being left behind in the region, with huge defense budgets sapping its economy.

sardonic   sar•DON•ik
(sarcastic)

Sardonic jokes about food stamps are wearing thin among faculty and other staff members who received their last pay checks in April.

sartorial   sar•TOR•ee•ull
(pertaining to clothing or dress, esp. men's)

Mr. Jordan's strongest initial impact on the capital may have been sartorial. He customarily appeared at all but the most formal occasions in a Navy peacoat, open-necked shirt, blue jeans and usually a pair of ankle-high boots.

scenario   suh•NAR•ee•oh
(an outline for any proposed or planned series of events, real or imagined)

According to Dr. Grey's scenario, on July 4, 2076, people from Earth will make the first landing on a planet beyond the solar system.

scion   SIGH•un
(descendant)

It's not surprising that Lois Burpee has achieved a reputation as a cook. She's the wife of a scion of the seed company whose sprouts have nourished more than a couple of generations of Americans.

scotch   SKOCH
(to put an end to)

And last week Saudi Crown Prince Fahd scotched oil industry hopes for a 40 percent increase in Saudi oil production that would have made up for cutbacks by Iran.

scourge   SKURJ
(a cause of serious trouble, affliction or calamity)

"Kondos," or armed thieves, have long been a scourge of Uganda.

scowl   SKOWL
(an angry or threatening frown)

McEnroe's face was the source of countless scowls and grimaces, accompanied by angry muttering when his cross-court shots missed by inches or when he wasn't getting in his first serves.

scrutinize   SKROOT•en•ize
(examine closely)

"Open trials," Justice Blackmun wrote, "enable the public to scrutinize the performance of police and prosecutors in the conduct of public judicial business."

sectarian   sek•TER•ee•un
(limited to a particular sect or religion)

The nonsectarian status of the college is important because it entitles the 100-year-old school to $2.25 million a year in state aid, which under state education law and the State Constitution cannot be given to a sectarian institution.

secular   SEK•yuh•lur
(relating to things that are worldly rather than religious)

Mayor Kollek said later: "I've tried for 13 years to keep the religious and secular communities in a spirit of coexistence."

sedentary   SED•en•ter•ee
(keeping one seated much of the time)

He eats lunch at his desk and has taken up jogging to counter the effects of long hours of sedentary work.

seer
(prophet)   SEER

Seers were predicting that if Boston swept the series, Billy Martin would be fired.

seething
(boilingly angry)   SEETH•ing

"Nobody in New York likes me," Reginald M. Jackson said in one of his more seething moments last week.

self-effacing
(minimizing one's own actions; modest)   self•ef•FAY•sing

Simms seems to take his status in stride. He is neither self-effacing nor boastful. He says he threw the ball well in high school and doesn't understand the lack of interest in him by college scouts.

sequester
(to keep separate and secure)   se•KWES•tur

Under the Freedom of Information Act, adopted in 1967 and substantially toughened by Congress in 1974, even a foreigner can petition for files sequestered in the Pentagon, the State Department and the C.I.A.

seraph
(an angel)   SER•uf

As the lunatic playing a triangle, Mr. Auberjonois has a look that is at the same time seraphic and soulful.

sere
(dry; withered)   SEER

The traditional Papago diet consists of pinto beans, tortillas and jelly made from the fruit of the saguaro cactus. ("Papago" means "bean people," a name applied by the neighboring Pima Indians in reference to one of the few foods that can grow on this sere land.)

serene
(calm; untroubled; tranquil)   suh•REEN

Mr. Giscard d'Estaing now seems to fit comfortably into his elegant palace and seems confident and serene.

servile
SER•vile
(like a slave; humbly yielding; submissive)
There also appears to have been some in-fighting and discussion in Spanish television, one of the least imaginative and politically servile organizations in the country, about showing "Holocaust."

simplistic
sim•PLISS•tik
(making complex problems unrealistically simple; oversimplified)
The television series, "Holocaust," was criticized by some in the United States as simplistic, but in Europe and especially West Germany, it was a powerful, if unwanted, reminder of Nazi atrocities.

simulate
SIM•yuh•late
(to have the appearance of)
Police said that although the simulated revolver could not be fired, they could not be positive that a real gun had not been used in the attempted robbery.

sine qua non
SIGH•nee•kway•NAHN
(an essential condition)
Long before they turned up in this show, these pictures had achieved that hold over people's minds and imginations which is—or should be—the sine qua non of a true work of art.

slipshod
SLIP•SHOD

(careless)

At the Miami airport early today, dozens of worried relatives and friends of people aboard the hijacked jetliner waited anxiously for word on their return. Some expressed anger over what they called slipshod airline security.

slough
SLUFF

(to shed)

David Bowie sloughs off musical styles and theatrical personas like a snake sheds its skin.

snafu
sna•FOO

(an acronym for "situation normal: all fouled up"; a mix-up or muddled situation)

He is rarely flustered. He can handle technical snafus with incomparable skill and considerable humor.

snipe
SNIPE

(to criticize, esp. from a safe distance)

The predominately Democratic Western governors took aim at the White House today, sniping at the Carter Administration's policies on wilderness, water and rangeland.

sobriquet
SO•bri•kay

(a nickname)

The nattily attired "Park Avenue Bandit" knocked over five Manhattan banks in the last two months, deriving his sobriquet from the three stickups he staged at Citibank branches on Park Avenue.

solace
SAH•lis

(comfort; consolation)

Tammy Mathre was obsessed with the rugged high country of Wyoming and the solace it offered from a 20-year-old's troubles.

solecism SOL•uh•siz•um
(a grammatical error)
His English is full of solecisms, but the ideas and emotions come streaming out with the vivid, poignant, colored, tender vitality of his music.

solicitous suh•LI•suh•tuhs
(showing care, attention or concern)
But was it really necessary for Secretary General Waldheim to be so solicitous of Vietnam's feelings that he tried to stifle direct verbal attacks on what Vietnam has done?

somber SOM•bur
(causing serious thoughts)
The Chancellor began his speech with a somber review of the economy. Inflation was rising rapidly again, he said, imports were high because domestic industry could not turn out the goods, and consumer spending rose far more than manufacturing output last year.

sophisticated suh•FIS•tuh•kate•ud
(highly complex or developed)
To counter that advantage, the South Koreans want sophisticated weapons and the best technology that the United States will sell them.

soporific sop•uh•RIF•ik
(sleep-inducing)
The Tanner-DuPre match was the first time the two men had played each other. Their match bordered on the soporific, with long rallies of good but not scintillating tennis.

spare SPARE
(scanty)
Michael did the décor—witty and spare with a tubular steel staircase spiraling to the second floor.

spartan SPAR•tuhn
(rigorously simple; unluxurious)
Despite the Senator's prominence in Washington, he maintained a spartan weekend lifestyle on his 90-acre farm in Dover, 15 miles south of Boston, where he clad his gangling frame in work clothes, mowed grass, milked cows, sawed wood and looked after his 1,600 chickens.

spate SPATE
(a flood or sudden heavy rain)
There has been a spate of arrests since then, and some investigators admit that the captured files have been useful in putting together new cases.

spawn SPAWN
(to give birth to)
Flash floods spawned by heavy rains battered a mountainous region of southeastern Kentucky yesterday, killing at least two people and forcing hundreds to leave their homes, the authorities said.

specter SPEK•tur
(an object of fear or dread)
Mr. Bell and his immediate predecessor, Edward H. Levi, are widely credited with restoring morale and integrity, but the specter of political interference still haunts the department.

spectrum SPEK•trum
(a broad range)
Mr. Tugwell held the title of Assistant Secretary of Agriculture in the early years of the New Deal, but he advised Mr. Roosevelt on a wide spectrum of policies for recovery from the Depression.

spoof SPOOF
(to satirize in a playful manner)
"Scrambled Feet" spoofs the theatre world, from ac-

tors and agents to directors, theatregoers, producers, composers and playwrights.

sporadic   spuh•RAD•ik
(scattered)

There were reports of strike-related violence in at least 12 states today, including sporadic shootings, firebombings and rock-throwing incidents.

spurious   SPYUR•ee•us
(false; counterfeit)

A number of spurious bomb warnings led to chaos this morning in the Madrid subway system, which was briefly emptied and searched.

spurn   SPURN
(to refuse or reject)

Fears of ballooning expenditures and logistical headaches have turned the Olympics into an international pariah in the last few years, with more and more cities and countries spurning the chance to play host to the athletes.

squalid   SKWOL•id
(wretched; miserable)

Twice in the 15-year history of the squalid tent settlement the people have been bulldozed out by the municipal authorities, who had other plans for the land. Both times the people came back.

squander   SKWON•dur
(to spend or use wastefully)

Ghana's former head of state, Ignatius K. Acheampong, was executed by firing squad early today after being convicted of squandering Government funds.

squelch   SKWELCH
(to suppress or silence in a crushing way)

"It's unbelievable. Nicaragua has never had democracy and it's been the United States which has squelched attempts to create it."

static STA•tik
(lacking movement or vitality)
(9) Movie: "Tales of Hoffman" (1953). Moira Shearer, Robert Rounseville, Robert Helpman. Stylish, static serving of the opera by the "Red Shoes" crew, minus the magic. Fine listening, but a royal bore to watch. (2 hrs.)

steadfast STED•fast
(unwavering; firm)
Mississippians have steadfastly opposed attempts by Federal agencies to store similar nuclear waste in underground salt domes along the Gulf Coast.

stereotype STER•ee•uh•tipe
(a fixed notion about a person or group, held by a number of people, and allowing for no individuality)
"Many women believe that in order to be effective they are expected to restrict their public behavior to traditional feminine stereotypes," she said. "Thus women are supposed to be softspoken, passive and genteel."

stern STURN
(strict)
"You feel like a little kid who's done something wrong," says Harry Carson, the middle linebacker, "and he's your daddy giving you that stern parental glare."

stigma
(mark of disgrace)   STIG•muh

Locating work for these women is difficult, she said, "because there is a social stigma attached to women who've spent time in prison."

stipulate
(to require as an essential condition in making an agreement)   STIP•yuh•late

The treaty stipulates that neither the surface nor subsurface of the moon shall become any country's national property.

stoic
(emotionally unmoving; unimpassioned)   STO•ik

Unsmiling stoicism marked the characterization of Jay Silverheels when he played Tonto, the Lone Ranger's faithful Indian companion, on television, but Mr. Silverheels wept at ceremonies yesterday at which he became the first American Indian to have a star in his honor placed in the Hollywood Walk of Fame.

stolid
(unemotional; impassive)   STAH•lid

In the first "Rocky," the beating "The Italian Stallion" takes and the one he inflicts, while losing with stolid gallantry to champion Apollo Creed (Carl Weathers), are too severe for verisimilitude—in life neither man could have survived so many great hits.

strident
(harsh-sounding; shrill)   STRIDE•ent

We now see the "new" Carter—strident, loud, fist-clenching on cue, the preacher threatening hellfire and damnation.

subservient
(submissive)   sub•SUR•vee•unt

The influence of the Chiefs on Capitol Hill has waned

somewhat in recent years, with conservatives suggesting that they have become too subservient to the White House.

subsidiary   sub•SID•ee•er•ee
(a company whose controlling interest is owned by another company)

The Canada Dry Corporation, a subsidiary of Norton Simon Inc., thinks the time has come for an almost-caffeine-free cola.

substantive   SUB•stun•tiv
(essential)

Senator Frank Church, Democrat of Idaho, said tonight that it would be a "grave mistake" for the Senate to adopt substantive changes in the treaty.

succinct   suk•SINGKT
(clearly and briefly stated)

Congressman Jack Kemp put it succinctly: "The only reason we have gas lines in parts of the country is that it is illegal today to match up willing suppliers with willing consumers of gasoline."

succulent   SUK•yuh•lunt
(juicy)

Aphids or plant lice cluster and feed on the young succulent shoots of many flower and vegetable plants.

succumb   suh•KUM
(yield)

Ever since his troops drove Idi Amin from Uganda, President Julius K. Nyerere of Tanzania has been resisting the temptation to run both countries. Last week there were signs he might be succumbing.

suffice   suh•FICE
(to be sufficient)

He was beloved because he did not leave Boston when

success opened the way, as so many others have done and because he took its name with him all over the world as "Arthur Fiedler of the Boston Pops" when "Arthur Fiedler" would have sufficed.

suffuse suh•FYOOZ
(to overspread)

Since the tall Gothic church was built over a century ago, it has been the center of the quiet village and within its walls the lives of the people have been suffused with the rituals and teachings of the Roman Catholic faith.

summary SUM•uh•ree
(hasty and arbitrary)

Meanwhile, some 40 reporters, including all but one employee of the three major United States television networks, have left the country following the summary killing Wednesday of an ABC-TV correspondent, Bill Stewart, by a National Guardsman.

superficial soo•pur•FISH•ull
(shallow)

The fact is that good wines come from bad years and bad wines from good years. A lot of superficial knowledge about vintages has nothing to do with the true value of the wine.

superfluous soo•PUR•flu•wuss
(needless)

As the students born during the post-World War II "baby boom" have grown up, passed through their public-school systems and graduated, the hundreds of buildings erected to accommodate them and the thousands of teachers hired to instruct them have become superfluous.

supersede soo•pur•SEED
(to take the place of; cause to be obsolete)

It used to be that the expert on, say, what makes a

good breakfast was your mother. But all that has changed. With today's concern over carcinogens and cholesterol, not to mention calories, motherly wisdom has been superseded by the nutritionist's dictums.

surreptitious sur•ep•TISH•es
(acting in a secret or stealthy way)

Until now, the agency's responsibility was only to assure that commercial and research reactors were not used surreptitiously to produce nuclear weapons.

surrogate SER•uh•git
(substitute)

With the youngsters, Mrs. Johnson often assumes a posture of surrogate mother, disciplinarian, and, as she likes to put it, "educational leader."

sustenance SUS•tuh•nunts
(support; nourishment)

Although she was not frightened, she worried continually about being physically assaulted. She drew sustenance, she said, from her Roman Catholic faith and prayer.

swarthy SWOR•thee
(dark-complexioned)

Instead there's a slick, four-color poster on the wall showing a swarthy, barechested male wearing a pair of Jordache jeans.

symbiotic sim•bigh•AH•tik
(interdependent)

Most of the guards, loocked in a symbiotic relationship with their wards, are patient and occasionally even sympathetic.

synthesis SIN•thuh•sus
(a whole made up of parts or elements put together)

"A synthesis of all the universal musical forms."

That's how Joseph Jarmen, the reed player with the Art Ensemble of Chicago, describes his group's special sound.

tabloid　　　　　　　　　　　　TAB•loyd
(a newspaper, usually half the ordinary size, with many pictures and short, often sensational news stories)

Being her very first Wimbledon, Miss Siegel had no previous introduction to the daily British tabloids until the following day when her picture was exposed across the front page of several papers.

taboo　　　　　　　　　　　　ta•BOO
(a social prohibition or restriction)

In California, with the greatest concentration of nude beaches and, some say, the fewest taboos, the state is considering a plan to designate eight beaches on public land as "clothing optional."

tacit　　　　　　　　　　　　TAS•it
(unspoken; implied)

He singled out ABC because it announced that it would voluntarily cut commercial time in children's programming. "It is tacit admission that there's something wrong with advertising to children," he said.

taciturn　　　　　　　　　　　　TAS•i•turn
(almost always silent; not liking to talk; uncommunicative)

Sergio Ramirez Mercado, the taciturn 36-year-old leader of the junta, received the news at the Venezuelan Embassy, then drove home to greet well-wishers with his wife.

tacky
TAK•ee

(in poor taste)

Though some of this enthusiasm is taken to tacky extremes, such as lamps made of plastic Shakespeare heads, it indicates the town's well-deserved pride in its annual summer festival of Shakespearean plays.

tantamount
TAN•tuh•mount

(equal)

The last recommendation, opponents say, would be tantamount to permitting a full-scale resumption of bribery.

tarmac
TAR•mak

(an airport runway paved with a mixture of crushed stone and tar)

When Augusto Cesar Sandino was murdered in 1934 by Anastasio Somoza Garcia, the first Somoza, his body was hastily buried under the tarmac of Managua Airport.

taut
TAWT

(showing strain; tense)

In the first few days of the Wimbledon fortnight even the most steadfast nerves can get taut, so demanding is tennis on grass.

tax   TAKS
(put a strain on)

As a result of the fighting in Cambodia, thousands of Cambodians have poured into neighboring Thailand in recent months, taxing its refugee facilities.

tedious   TEE•dee•us
(tiresome)

Reid Anderson so overplayed Mercutio's jestings that his monkeyshines grew tedious.

teetotaler   TEE•tote•lur
(one who completely abstains from alcoholic drinks)

He always was a teetotaler, and he gave up sex after he and his wife, Gajraben, had five children.

tempestuous   tem•PES•choo•uhs
(turbulent; tumultuous)

An acrimonious weeklong conference of third-world nations ended quietly early this morning, a day late, after a tempestuous last negotiating session in which the frustrated Sri Lanka chairman reportedly threatened to resign.

temporal   TEM•puh•rull
(worldly)

Traditionally, the Dalai Lama, whose name means Ocean of Wisdom, exercised both spiritual and temporal power in Tibet.

tenacity   tuh•NAS•ut•ee
(firmness in holding fast; stubbornness; persistence)

Her family marveled at her tenacity: "You couldn't beat her down; I would have given up a million times," said her sister, Anita Berliawsky.

tender
TEN•dur
(present for acceptance; offer)

My Dear Mr. President: I hereby tender my resignation as United States Secretary of Transportation.

tenet
TEN•et
(a principle, document or belief held as a truth)

Why does the press report personal details when the right of an individual to privacy is such a cherished tenet in our society?

tentative
TEN•tuh•tiv
(hesitant or uncertain)

There, in flickering black and white on their television screens, they saw a man at the bottom rung of a ladder extend his booted left foot to touch, tentatively at first, then firmly, the gray powdery surface of the moon.

tenuous
TEN•yuh•wus
(unsubstantial; weak)

Further, studies have shown that a large proportion of the participants, like Miss Walton, are finding their way back to Judaism after a tenuous relationship to their religious heritage, or none at all.

tenure
TEN•yur
(the length of time something is held)

For someone who had always been in the visitors' dugout in New York before, Bob Lemon earned the ultimate tribute during his brief tenure as the Yankees' manager — instant admiration and affection.

terse
TURSS
(concise; succinct)

A terse announcement from the office of Jody Powell, the White House press secretary, reads as follows: "The President has decided to skip a planned vacation in Hawaii to return to Washington for Congressional

testy
TES•tee

(irritable; impatient; touchy)

Mr. Kuznetsov's defection came as a surprise in Soviet literary circles, where it had been assumed he was a loyal, if a bit testy, member of the establishment.

theologian
the•uh•LO•jen

(a specialist in the study of God, religious doctrines and matters of divinity)

Though many of the conflicts between scientists and theologians have been largely overcome, the goal of forming a partnership to meet human needs is still in the beginning stages.

thwart
THWORT

(to prevent from accomplishing a purpose; frustrate; defeat)

Arts and Letters, historians will recall, was the spoiler who thwarted Majestic Prince's bid in 1969 for the Triple Crown by beating him in the Belmont Stakes.

timorous
TIM•uh•russ

(timid)

Lt. Col. Bernardino Larios noted that President Carter had committed himself to human rights but said he thought the President was being too timorous in the case of Nicaragua.

topography
tuh•POG•ruh•fee

(the surface features of a region)

A topographical map of Manhattan on his office wall dating back to 1865 shows the original locations of the streams, swamps and rock outcroppings that once dominated the farmlands of midtown.

torpor
TOR•pur

(sluggishness)

They are easy to spot. They are often well dressed, even in the torpor of the tropics, with suits that are somehow always pressed.

tortuous   TOR•choo•wuss
(full of twists, turns, curves or windings)
Their forces would have to move over one or two tortuous routes: from the Balkans to Basra in Iraq by way of the Bosporus and Baghdad or, a shorter route, from the Caucasus to Kuwait.

tout   TOWT
(to praise or recommend highly)
Already home computers can retrieve information from data networks, while the pioneers in the videodisk industry are touting their system's ability to store an encyclopedia of information on a single record.

trajectory   truh•JEK•tu•ree
(the curved path of something hurtling through space)
The second Voyager's trajectory is such that it will encounter the four major moons during its approach to Jupiter rather than on the outward passage, as done by Voyager 1.

tranquil   TRAN•kwel
(peaceful; calm)
Over the last 11 years the public meetings of the Rent Guidelines Board have not been tranquil. But emotions at recent meetings, especially last Wednesday's, rose to new heights.

transcend   trans•END
(go beyond the limits of)
Increasingly, in states and municipalities around the country, the issue is creating rival groups, groups whose points of view transcend labels of Democrat and Republican, conservative and liberal.

transitory
trans•uh•TORE•ee
(short-lived; brief)

A job at the top in retailing these days is starting to look as transitory as coaching professional baseball.

transmogrify
trans•MOG•ruf•fie
(to transform, esp. in a strange or grotesque manner)

But it has lately become commonplace to find awful novels transmogrified into movies that are even worse, and surely this is a phenomenon worth looking into.

trepidation
trep•uh•DAY•shun
(fearful uncertainty)

At that meeting, many gas-station attendants expressed trepidation over abuse and threats from customers irate over long lines, about limits on purchases and line-jumping on the part of other customers.

TREPIDATION

trilogy
TRILL•uh•jee
(a set of three related plays, novels, etc., which together form an extended unified work, though each has its own unity)

Stallone sees "Rocky II" as the middle part of a trilogy.

truncate
TRUN•kate
(to shorten by cutting off a part)

Vacations by private car can be risky in a period of gasoline shortages. And the Government's grounding of the DC-10, one of the airline workhorses, puts immense new pressures on air travel. Other than the truncated railroads, all that's left is the bus.

turgid   TUR•jid
(pompous; bombastic)
One Western businessman told of submitting a letter in English to one ministry and receiving a reply in such turgid Arabic that even his Egyptian staff could not make sense of it.

turmoil   TUR•moil
(commotion; confusion; tumult; disorder)
Theatre in Latin America, in particular, is closely related to the socio-political realities of its countries, many of which live in political turmoil and most of which are under military dictatorships.

U

ubiquitous   yoo•BIK•wut•us
(present everywhere)
The ubiquitous pigeons came to this country in the 1700's with the earliest settlers. They were brought either as pets or to carry messages for the military.

unabashedly   un•uh•BASH•ud lee
(unashamedly)
Some plant lovers unabashedly admitted talking and even pleading with their plants.

UNABASHEDLY

uncanny un•KAN•ee
(beyond the normal; extraordinary)
She had a famous chop volley and an uncanny court sense that made her one of the most popular doubles partners.

unconscionable un•KONCH•uh•nuh•bull
(not guided by conscience; unscrupulous)
Some people feel that the reports on the death of Nelson A. Rockefeller, the former Vice President, constituted an unconscionable invasion of privacy, disclosing intimate details that were none of the public's business.

unequivocal un•i•KWIV•uh•kull
(leaving no trace of doubt; unambiguous)
"If there was one thing that the President was clear and unequivocal about, it was wage and price controls — he's not for them and we're not going to have them."

unflappable un•FLAP•uh•bull
(not easily excited, confused or alarmed; imperturbable)
Mr. Smith has won a reputation as energetic and unflappable, a low-key man who gets the job done.

unilateral yoo•nih•LAT•uh•rull
(one-sided)
"Just because I have taken over an agency with the word 'disarmament' in it doesn't mean I believe in unilateral disarmament."

unobtrusive   un·ub·TROO·siv
(not calling attention to oneself; inconspicuous)

For more than an hour, Ron Nickle stood unobtrusively near the back of the small, dirty-green union hall here, his arms crossed over his low-slung stomach and his florid face growing increasingly dour.

unprepossessing   un·pree·puh·ZESS·ing
(not notably impressive at first meeting, hearing, etc.)

Before he was catapulted, all unprepared, into the ranks of the superstars with the live album, he was a nice, unprepossessing British rocker.

unquantifiable   un·kwon·tih·FIE·uh·bull
(unmeasurable)

But there remains the unquantifiable worry about the damage done to the DC-10 in the minds of travelers.

unscathed   un·SKATHD
(unharmed)

Mr. Bonventre and Mr. Amato, who were at the same table on the patio, escaped unscathed and sped off in a 1977 blue Lincoln, according to witnesses.

upbraid   up·BRADE
(to scold severely)

Many of his customers had begun lining up hours before the station opened, and a Canadian who had unwittingly entered the station from the wrong side was heatedly upbraided.

urbane   ur·BANE
(polite and courteous in a smooth, polished way)

Cole Porter and Philip Barry stand as twin pinnacles of urbane sophistication in the 20's and 30's.

vacillate VAS•uh•late
(to show indecision; waver)
"The biggest criticism of our foreign policy is vacillation, not knowing where we are or where we're going."

vagaries vuh•GAIR•eez
(unpredictable occurrence)
"Barney Miller" began as standard domestic sit-com but has evolved into a clever commentary on urban vagaries.

valid VAL•id
(well-grounded; sound)
Q. *Do you know that old trick about spinning an egg to see if it is raw or hard-cooked?*
A. It is not a trick, but a perfectly valid method of determining which is which.

vehement VEE•uh•munt
(strongly emotional; intense or passionate)
When umpire Nick Bremigan called Bobby Murcer out at first on a close play in the sixth inning, Martin raced from the dugout to lodge a vehement protest and promptly incurred his first ejection since he returned to manage the Yankees.

vehicle VEE•ik•ull
(a play thought of as a means of presenting a specified actor)
Mr. Miller himself has a new musical that is supposed to be on Broadway next season, and he is working on a new play. He says it would be a fine vehicle for Kim Stanley.

venality
vee•NA•luh•tee
(openness to bribery or corruption)

Long before taking on the giant I.G. Farben concern in a book published last summer, Mr. Borkin examined venality and dishonesty in the judiciary in a book entitled "The Corrupt Judge."

vendetta
ven•DET•uh
(a prolonged feud or seeking for vengeance)

The Chagra family sees the charges against Jimmy Chagra as merely the most recent manifestation of a Government vendetta that began 10 years ago, when the Justice Department first began trying to prove that Lee Chagra was a major controller of narcotics traffic.

veneer
vuh•NEER
(an attractive but superficial appearance)

(2) MOVIE: "Executive Suite" (1954). William Holden, Fredric March, Barbara Stanwyck, June Allyson, Paul Douglas. Swank cast, big business intrigue, shiny veneer, strictly surface. But entertaining (1 hr. 58 mins.)

venerable
VEN•ur•uh•bull
(held in respect because of age, dignity, character, position, etc.)

The Olivers and a score of other hollerers of all ages gathered here to meet old friends, swap techniques and, mainly, to holler. It is a venerable tradition here and in a few other rural hamlets, born of necessity in the days before the telephone and the CB radio.

veracity
vuh•RA•suh•tee
(truth)

The broadcast, whose veracity cannot be ascertained, was the first word that has reached the outside world of the fate of the refugees.

verbatim vur•BATE•um
(word for word)
With her colleagues, she is an affable but firm administrator who frequently punctuates her speech with verbatim quotations from teacher contracts and legislative statutes.

verbiage VER•bee•ij
(wordiness)
The California Governor's cynical opportunism and flaky verbiage have made him a figure of mockery lately among political commentators.

verdant VURD•ent
(green)
The giant machine rumbled over the verdant Salinas Valley, huffing and puffing. There were 20 farmhands aboard the machine and today they harvested 110 tons of tomatoes, an average of 5.5 tons per worker.

verisimilitude ver•uh•suh•MIL•uh•tood
(the appearance of being true or real)
The film's scenes of nighttime close combat have a verisimilitude lacking in many more ambitious films.

vex VEKS
(to trouble or distress)
The problem of controlling crowds at popular museum shows is one that vexes museum officials the world over.

viable VIE•uh•bull
(able to healthfully survive or grow)
"Those who wrote New York off in the mid-70's were wrong," he added. "There is not a stronger, more viable location in the world than midtown Manhattan."

vicarious vie•KAR•ee•us
(felt or shared through imagined participation in the experience of others)

Many parents live vicariously through their children. When their child succeeds or wins, parents view this as a personal victory. If the child is unsuccessful, parents interpret this as a reflection on their ability as a mother or father.

vicissitudes   vuh•SIS•uh•toodz
(unpredictable changes)

In mid-1970, he began to recommend gold issues as a hedge against inflation and the vicissitudes of the stock market.

vilification   vil•uh•fuh•KAY•shun
(abusive or slanderous language)

New York City's Health and Hospitals Corporation ignored vilifications and threats yesterday and wisely backed Mayor Koch's plan to shrink the municipal hospital system.

vindicate   VIN•duh•kate
(to clear from blame, criticism, guilt, suspicion, etc.)

Later, as he happily pushed through the crowds outside, a free man again, Mr. Thorpe called the verdict "totally fair, just, and a complete vindication."

virtually   VIR•choo•well•ee
(for all practical purposes; just about)

And there is not a single black or Asian member of the House of Commons. In the last election, five nonwhite candidates ran, with the nominations of major parties, but in all districts in which they ran, they had virtually no chance of winning.

virulent   VIR•yuh•lunt
(malignant or deadly)

"And the doctors kept saying Connie was a very young man to have such virulent cancer."

visage
(face) — VIZ•ij

The dominant image of Dr. Marcuse, with his sensitive eyes, high forehead and weathered visage, was of a solitary figure who felt most at home with his books.

visceral
(emotional, rather than intellectual; gut) — VIS•uh•rul

However, Mr. Bradley said, "my visceral reaction is the revelations are going to get worse." He added that "we haven't heard the end of this."

vitriolic
(extremely sharp and bitter) — vi•tree•OL•ik

At times, the debate reached the heights of vitriolic silliness, but passions run high in the architectural world.

vituperative
(verbally abusive and bitter) — vie•TOO•puh•rut•iv

William Loeb, whose conservative views and often vituperative editorials as publisher of the Manchester Union Leader have influenced the conduct of Presidential primaries in New Hampshire for decades, agreed today to settle a suit charging pension law violations on terms that will cause him to lose control of 25 percent of the newspaper's stock.

volatile
(not lasting long; unstable; fleeting) — VOL•uh•tul

The editor's position at Newsweek has been a volatile one in recent years. Mr. Bernstein becomes the fourth person to hold the job since 1969.

voluminous
(of ample size, extent or fullness) — vuh•LOO•muh•nuhs

Draped in a voluminous brown corduroy gown, she rises from her chair and paces up and down.

vulnerable   VUHL•nuh•ruh•buhl
(open to attack; defenseless)
After hostile receptions in populated ports, many Vietnamese appear to be beaching their vulnerable boats on obscure islands in a bid for at least temporary shelter and survival.

watershed   WOT•ur•SHED
(a crucial turning point between two phases)
Dr. Billington has concluded that the 1970's are a watershed decade, the decade that future historians will judge to be the one in which values stemming from the American frontier began yielding to European ones.

white elephant   hwight EL•uh•fuhnt
(a possession unwanted by the owner but difficult to dispose of)
That's not to say that the real-estate agents weren't tempted to do so, especially since the 40-year-old house was beginning to look like a white elephant, having drawn no buyers for more than a year after being put up for sale at an asking price of $1 million.

wily   WHY•lee
(crafty; sly)
One wily farmer promised an Indian a bushel basket of cider for his services.

wistful
(longing; yearning)

WIST·ful

Murata and Hana talk wistfully about going home, but know it is not likely to happen.

wrench
(to twist or pull suddenly and violently; wrest)

RENCH

Nevada has made a move to wrench most of its land from Federal control.

wry
(disdainfully ironic or amusing)

RIE

And Robert Boris, "Blood Feud's" co-author, says wryly, "I spent a year and a library card finding out what it took the committee two and a half years and $5 million to discover."

Z

zealous
(intensely enthusiastic or devoted)

ZEL·us

A church group whose zealous praise of the Lord resulted in a $532 fine for disturbing the peace said today that its constitutional rights to freedom of religion and speech had been violated.

Credits

Samuel Abt
Virginia Adams
William J. Alexander
John H. Allan
David M. Alpern
Lawrence K. Altman
Neil Amdur
Jack Anderson
Susan Heller Anderson
David A. Andelman
Dave Anderson
Frederick Andrews
R.W. Apple, Jr.
Karen W. Arenson
Anthony Austin
B. Drummond Ayres, Jr.
Russell Baker
Josh Barbanel
J.C. Barden
James Barron
Barbara Basler
William Bates
Janet Battaile
Paul Belinkie
Leslie Bennetts
David Binder
David Bird
Maryann Bird
Mark Blackburn
J.F. Blake
Roy Blount
Deborah Blumenthal
Ralph Blumenthal
William Borders
Andrew Borowiec
James Bovard
Donald D. Breed
Kenneth A. Briggs
Jane E. Brody
Malcolm W. Browne
Anatole Broyard
Yale Brozen
Nadine Brozan
Nelson Bryant
Tom Buckley
David Burnham
John F. Burns
Richard Burt
Fox Butterfield
Robert Byrne
Steve Cady
Vincent Canby
Father Ernesto Cardenal
Deirdre Carmody
Maurice Carroll
Linda Charlton
Murray Chass
Tony Chiu

Craig Claiborne
Alfred E. Clark
Andrew Clark
Francis X. Clines
Adam Clymer
Joan Cook
John Corry
John M. Crewdson
Ann Crittenden
David Crosen
Judith Cummings
Lee A. Daniels
John Darnton
Alvin Davis
Peter Davis
Karen DeWitt
E.J. Dionne, Jr.
Greg Donaldson
Philip H. Dougherty
Georgia Dullea
Gerald Dumas
Jennifer Dunning
Joseph Durso
Richard Eder
James Egan
D.D. Eisenberg
Ken Emerson
Raymond Ericson
Gerald Eskenazi
Barbara Ettorre
Meryle Evans
Clyde H. Farnsworth
Joan Lee Faust
Tom Ferrell
Gordon F. Foster
Glenn Fowler
Pierre Franey
Gerald Fraser
Milt Freudenheim
Jane Friedman
Nicholas Gage
Barbara Gamerekian
Henry Giniger
Grace Glueck
Paul Goldberger
George Goldman, Jr.
Linda Greenhouse
Paul Grimes
Jane Gross
Pranay B. Gupte
Mel Gussow
Bernard Gwertzman
Clyde Haberman
Richard Halloran
Robert Hanley
Aljean Harmetz
Thomas C. Hayes
Fred M. Hechinger

John Herbers
Robin Herman
Robert D. Hershey, Jr.
Donald G. Herzberg
Richard Higgins
Norman Hildes-Heim
Gladwin Hill
Robert S. Hillman, M.D.
Sheila M. Hillman
Michael de Courcy Hinds
Christopher Hitchens
Roy B. Hoffman
Paul Hofmann
Warren Hoge
Ron Hollander
Ernest Holsendolph
Paul F. Horvitz
Marvine Howe
Allen Hughes
Ada Louise Huxtable
Youssef M. Ibrahim
Molly Ivins
David Jarmul
Sharon Johnson
Thomas S. Johnson
Laurie Johnston
Brendan Jones
Stacy V. Jones
Charles Kaiser
Robert Blair Kaiser
Henry Kamm
Jonathan Kandell
Michael Katz
Michael Kaufman
Shawn G. Kennedy
Walter Kerr
Parton Keese
John Kifner
Seth S. King
Anna Kisselgoff
Wayne King
Dena Kleiman
N.R. Kleinfield
Judy Klemesrud
Allan Kozinn
Michael Knight
Hilton Kramer
Albin Krebs
Thomas Lask
Melvin J. Lasky
Carol Lawson
Christopher Lehmann-Haupt
Anthony Lewis
Flora Lewis
Paul Lewis
Robert Lindsey
Arnold H. Lubasch
Frank Lynn

Richard D. Lyons
Leslie Maitland
Jack Manning
Joseph Margolis
James M. Markham
Janet Maslin
Edwin McDowell
Robert D. McFadden
George McGovern
Deane McGowen
Richard J. Meislin
Robert Metz
Karl E. Meyer
Drew Middleton
Judith Miller
Barbara Mitchell
Herbert Mitgang
Charles Mohr
Irvin Molotsky
Bernadine Morris
Rochelle Moss
Alison Muscatine
Enid Nemy
Christopher Nyerges
John J. O'Connor
Ulick O'Connor
Juan de Onis
Eric Pace
Robert Palmer
Anthony J. Parisi
Jacques Pepin
Iver Peterson
William Pfaff
Joanne Pottlitzer
Frank J. Prial
Selwyn Raab
John S. Radosta
Howell Raines
Steven Rattner
Robert Reinhold
James Reston
Reuters
Alan Richman
Alan Riding
William Robbins
Nan Robertson
Steven V. Roberts
John Rockwell
Thomas Rogers
Gene Rondinaro
Sheila Rule
John Russell
William Safire
Sandra Salmans
Wolfgang Saxon
Anne-Marie Schiro
Harold C. Schonberg
Edward Schumacher

Peter J. Schuyten
Tony Schwartz
William Serrin
Philip Shabecoff
Richard F. Shepard
Nathaniel Sheppard, Jr.
David K. Shipler
Leonard Silk
Mimi Sheraton
Barbara Slavin
Leonard Sloane
Hedrick Smith
Red Smith
Terence Smith
Ronald Smothers
James P. Sterba
Henry Scott Stokes
Michael Strauss
Reginald Stuart
Ronald Sullivan
Walter Sullivan
A.O. Sulzberger, Jr.
Henry Tanner
Kathleen Teltsch
Robert McG. Thomas, Jr.
Howard Thompson
Martin Tolchin
Samuel Tower

Robert Trumbull
Wallace Turner
Lawrence Van Gelder
Vartanig G. Vartan
George Vecsey
Alice Villadolid
John Vinocur
Martin Waldron
Alex Ward
Warren Weaver, Jr.
Bayard Webster
Bernard Weinraub
Steven R. Weisman
Patricia Wells
Alden Whitman
Craig R. Whitney
Tom Wicker
Phillip H. Wiggins
John Noble Wilford
Richard Witkin
Roger Wilkins
Winston Williams
John S. Wilson
Christopher S. Wren
Carey Winfrey
Michael Wright
Don Wycliff
Alex Yannis